To Sharlene Enjoy These

HISTORICAL

CHRISTMAS

COOKERY

recipes, Thanks & Have a

Favorite Christmas Recipes From
the Colonies and Revolutionary War
Through the Time of the Civil War.

Wonderful Christmas

Sincere regards,
Robert W Pelton
Mans Ken STATion
OcT 21, 2000

Robert W. Pelton

Copyright © 2003 by Robert W. Pelton

ISBN 0-7414-1088-5

Published by:

INFIИITY
PUBLISHING.COM

1094 New DeHaven Street, Suite 100
West Conshohocken, PA 19428-2713
Info@buybooksontheweb.com
www.buybooksontheweb.com
Toll-free (877) BUY BOOK
Local Phone (610) 941-9999
Fax (610) 941-9959

∞

Printed in the United States of America

Printed on Recycled Paper

Published November 2005

Part of the Pelton Historical

Cookbook Series.

Includes the Following Titles:

Historical Thanksgiving Cookery

Revolutionary War Period Cookery

Civil War Period Cookery

Covers Such Categories as:

Signers of the Declaration of Independence

Confederate Military Leaders

Foreign Friends of the American Revolution

Signers of Our Constitution

Union Military Leaders

Heroes of the War for Independence

Includes the Favorite Recipes of:

Nathan Hale

Benjamin Franklin

Robert E. Lee

Ethan Allen

Stonewall Jackson

Ulysses S. Grant

John Adams

George Washington

John S. Mosby

Jefferson Davis

John Paul Jones

Nathan Bedford Forrest

Dedication

To my early descendants, Barnabus Horton of Leichestershire, England, who sailed to America on the *Swallow* some time between 1633 and 1638 with his wife Mary and their two sons, Joseph and Benjamin. They landed at Hampton, Massachusetts, and were Puritans;

And also to my Great Great-grandmother Huldah Radike Horton, one of the finest and most famous horsewomen of her day. She rode with Lafayette in a parade in his honor in Newburg, New York, in 1824. The French General and friend of the young Republic was making his second and final visit.

Contents

Preface

There was once a law that actually banned the celebration of Christmas for 22 years. On May 11, 1659, in the Massachusetts Bay Colony, members of the legislature passed a law making all Christmas festivities illegal!

The anti-Christmas law was passed just four years after England had repealed a similar statute. It had proven to be extremely unpopular on this side of the Atlantic, just as it had been over there. Most people in the Colonies, regardless of their faith, wanted Christmas to be a day of gift giving, feasting and merrymaking.

The unique legislation was worded in part: *"Whosoever shall be found observing any such day as Christmas ... shall pay for every offence five shillings."*

Accordingly, a citizen was in serious trouble on Christmas day if he or she **"read common prayer, danced, played cards or played any musical instrument except the drum, trumpet, or jews harp."**

The Governor of the Massachusetts Bay Colony, William Bradford, admonished his people:*"We must take the sternest measures against this popish [catholic] day."*

Christmas day was to be solely devoted to hard labor. Bradford further found it necessary to rebuke the*"lusty young men"* in the Colony who chose *"to pitch ye barr, and play at stoole ball and such like sports"* on Christmas day.

One unbending old judge, Samuel Sewell, sternly warned those in the Colony not to sin by making minced pies or plum pudding over the holiday period. He vociferously proclaimed that women who committed such misdeeds would surely be *"cursed by God for eternity."*

The Massachusetts Bay Colony was this continent's stronghold of the Puritans, one of which was influential Robert Brown. He wrote: *"The day called Christmas really means Christ-Mass. It is of the devil!"*

To Brown and his associates, Christmas was no more than *"a popish frivolity"* at best, and *"the dreadful work of Satan"* in their midst, at worst. Highest on the list of intolerable things to a Puritan was any holiday smacking of Roman Catholicism. The logic? Hadn't Catholics celebrated Christmas for centuries? Was this not reason enough to condemn Christmas as a work of the devil?

According to Puritan John Burton Smythe, Christmas had to be outlawed in order *"to keep purity among the people."* And the ban would *"protect them from the wiles of the devil who has been known to be working in the hearts of many good people."*

Those Puritans in positions of authority believed the legislation was truly a necessity. Why? The law's preamble spells it out. It was designed *"for preventing disorders among the people."* And furthermore, it would *"prevent the observing of such festivals as were superstitiously kept in other countries to the great dishonor of God and the offense of others."*

Did the Colonial leadership finally rescind their Christmas prohibition? No! The harsh law remained in effect until 1681 until King Charles 11 and his Royal Commission stepped in and forced its repeal. Only then could Christmas finally be celebrated without suffering dire consequences in the Massachusetts Bay Colony.

Introducing Historical Christmas Cookery

Historical Christmas Cookery is chock full of delightfully delicious cooking ideas favored by many famous families of yesteryear. It contains the prized recipes for those Christmas dishes served and eaten by some of the early settlers in the American Colonies. Here will be found the favorite Yuletide dishes of some of the heroes of the Revolutionary War. You will be able to fix and then eat the same things served to those great men who so bravely signed the *Declaration of Independence* and those involved in writing and signing our great *Constitution*. You will be able to sample the identical food eaten at Christmas by those foreign heroes who volunteered to fight and die for our freedom. And lastly, you can enjoy sharing an identical Christmas meal with those who wore both the blue and the gray during the War Between the States, or as some unreconstructed Southerners still refer to it, the War of Northern Aggression.

Included are recipes for tasty Christmas breads and many other kinds of baked goods, really good meat and poultry dishes, soups and stews and stuffings – and, yes, even pickles as well as loads of other wonderful things.

Here you will also be treated to the Christmas favorites of such historical luminaries as *Declaration of Independence* signer, Elbridge Gerry, who dearly loved his poultry dishes accompanied by a special **Sausage Stuffing**. Or the **Hollandaise Sauce** enjoyed by John Quincy Adams with his cauliflower. And that special Christmas **Coffee Loaf Cake** made by the wife of the famed Confederate General, "Fighting Joe" Hooker.

Here for example is a very old recipe *"TO MAKE SPICE CAKES,"* an all-time favorite during the Christmas holidays in the Colonies and thereafter in early America. It was published around 400 years ago in **COUNTREY CONTENTMENTS: OR THE ENGLISH HOUSEWIFE** by Gervase Markham. A copy of this cook book was brought over to the Colonies by my Puritan ancestors, Barnabus and Mary Horton when they sailed from England to Massachusetts on the *Swallow*. Here's how the cake was made:

"To make excellent spice cakes, take halfe a pecke of very fine Wheat-flower, take almost one pound of sweet butter, and some good milke and creame mixt together, set it on the fire, and put in your butter, and a good deale of sugar, and let it melt together; then straine Saffron into your milke a good quantity; then take seven or eight spooneful of good Ale barme, and eight egges with two yelkes and mix them together, then put your milke to it when it is somewhat cold, and into your flower put salt, Aniseedes bruised, Cloves and Mace, and a good deale of Cinamon: then worke all together good and stiffe, that you

need not worke in any flower after; then put in a little rose water cold, then rub it well in the thing you knead it in, and worke it thoroughly: if it be not sweet enough, scrape in a little more sugar, and pull it all in peeces, and hurle in a good quantity of Currants, and so worke all together againe, and bake your Cake as you see cause in a gentle warme oven."

In 1742 Colonial Williamsburg, E. Smith came out with **THE COMPLEAT HOUSEWIFE: or ACCOMPLISH'D GENTLEWOMAN'S COMPANION**. Even in this case, the woman of the house was pretty much expected to know what to do when she read over the recipe since the instructions given were far from explicit. Note how the quantities in Smith's recipe are extremely vague. This old-time Christmas favorite, *"APPLE PASTRIES TO FRY"* went like this:

"Pare and quarter Apples, and boil them in Sugar and Water, and a Stick of Cinnamon, and when tender, put in a little White Wine, the Juice of a Lemon, a Piece of fresh Butter, and a little Ambergrease or Orange flavored Water; stir all together, and when 'tis cold, put it in Puff paste, and fry them."

Gingerbread was always a popular item served at the Christmas tables in the Colonies. Here's an original recipe for *"Ginger-Bread Cakes."* This one was published by Hannah Glasse in her 1747 **THE ART OF COOKERY MADE PLAIN AND EASY**:

"To make Ginger-Bread Cakes. Take three Pounds of Flour, one Pound of Sugar, one Pound

of Butter, rubbed in very fine, two Ounces of Ginger beat very fine, a large Nutmeg grated; then take a Pound of Treakle, a quarter of a Pint of cream, make them warm together, and make up the bread stiff, roll it out, make it up into thin Cakes, cut them out with a Teacup, or a small glass, or roll them round like Nuts, bake them on Tin Plates in a slack Oven." Author's note: (Treakle is molasses).

A Harvard College graduate in 1755, Sir John Wentworth was the Colonial Governor of New Hampshire from 1767 to 1775. Here is his personal recipe for the special onion soup he dearly loved to eat at Christmas. This was found carefully inscribed in an old ledger:

"Cut a plate full of thin slices of Bread, and sett them before ye fire to Crisp. Then cutt about half a Dozen of Midle Size Onions into bits, boyle half a pound of Butter Stiring it well till it be very red and have done frothing and then put ye Onions to it, and boyle them till they begin to turn Blackish, Still stiring of them, to this put

about 2 quarts of water, and thicken it with 2 yolks of Eggs, then break ye Bread into small pieces and put it in with Some Spice & a little Salt, when it is ready pour in some Lemon Juce, or a Spoonfull or two of Vinegar if ye like it."

Early American recipes, as originally written, are often extremely difficult, if not impossible to use today with any degree of ease or accuracy. Such recipes, as can be seen by the above examples, were for the most part, written as one long and rather complicated paragraph. Instructions as given were obscure to say the least, and the amounts of the ingredients were all so often left up to the homemaker. On the other hand, many old-time recipes were simply a list of ingredients with no directions as how to mix them, or in what particular order they were to be added. Take for example this old Christmas favorite found in **NEW AMERICAN COOKERY or FEMALE COMPANION** published in 1805 by An American Lady. The author offered this recipe for *"CHEAP SEED CAKE"*:

"Rub one pound of sugar, half an ounce of alspice into four quarts of flour, into which pour one pound of butter melted, in one pint of milk, nine eggs, one gill 'emptins' (carraway seeds and currants, or raisins if you please) make into two loaves, bake one and a half hours."

Many old baking recipes would call for certain types of yeast. It might be **German** or **Compressed Yeast, Patent Yeast, Brewers Yeast** or **Potato Yeast.** Some yeast was even made using grape leaves, other yeast was made using hops. Such recipes were made more practical for today's homemakers by simply substituting the more modern versions of yeast – those small packets we can readily purchase in any of our supermarkets.

A unique old-fashioned method for making yeast from grape leaves was handed down by my Great-great grandmother, Huldah Radike Horton. This is the recipe she used in making the bread she served to her family every Christmas for many years. And it was used to make the bread she served to General Lafayette (1757-1834) when she entertained him at her home in Newburg, New York in 1823. Here's how she wrote it down:

"YEAST FROM GRAPE LEAVES

"Grape leaves make a yeast in some respects superior to hops, as the bread made from it rises sooner, and has not the peculiar taste which many object to in that made from hops. Use eight or ten leaves for a quart of yeast; Boil them for ten minutes; Pour the hot liquor on the flour, the quantity of the latter being determined by whether the yeast is wanted thicke or thin; Use the hop-yeast to raise it with to begin with, and

afterwards that made of grape leaves. Dried leaves will be as good as fresh. If a dark film appears upon the surface when rising, a little stirring will obviate it."

Patrick Henry (1736-99) stood tall among heroes when America was in desperate need of unselfish, unafraid men to guide her destiny. He electrified the members of the Continental Congress in 1774 when he arose before them and boldly declared: ***"The distinctions between Virginians, Pennsylvanians, New Yorkers, and New Englanders are no more. I am not a Virginian, but an American!"*** This great patriot was but one of many devout Christians who were active in the founding of our great nation. It is little known that he often enjoyed roast turkey as prepared by his wife, Dorthea Dandridge Henry. Here is how she made it for her husband:

"After washing the Fowl and putting it in Salt Water to stand for some Hours, pour some hot Water into the Body of the Turkey to heat it well. Wipe it dry inside and out, then fill the Body and Breast of the Turkey with Dressing which has

already been made. For Dressing, prepare Bread in Quantity proportioned to the Size of the Fowl. A twelve-pound Turkey will require a Quart Loaf to stuff it properly; a small Hen only half as much. Break up the Bread between your Hands, mixing well with a Tablespoonful of Butter and Seasoning of black Pepper, Salt and a Teaspoonful of bruised Celery-seed; make the Dressing hold together with a little hot Water, or Yolk of an egg and water. After filling with the Dressing, sew it up, rub it all over with fine Salt, tie the Legs and Wings close down and put it to roast with a moderate fire. In about half an hour baste it all over with Butter and dust on the Flour. Do this three or four Times while roasting; it will make it look nice and brown. Pour the Gravy each time into a Bowl to keep it from burning. For a Turkey of about ten Pounds, roast about three Hours."

Measurements were given in the past in ways that present day cooks wouldn't be expected to be at all familiar. Who today for example, when busily scurrying around the kitchen, would be able to accurately measure out a teacupful, ½ a tincup, a dessertspoonful or butter the size of an egg when called for in a recipe? Now try butter the size of a walnut, a pound of eggs, a kitchencupful, or even a dram of liquid? Or how about half a tumbler, a saltspoonful, a wineglassful, a gill, or a pound of milk? Since this would create an insurmountable problem, all the recipes in **HISTORICAL CHRISTMAS COOKERY** have been carefully updated so that when the recipe is used today, it will turn out just as it did for the homemaker who prepared it for her family so many years ago. Here is a list of some of the more unusual items used by housewives of the past. The original measurement is given first just as she may have had to use it in one of her recipes. This is followed by today's updated version of the same item:

Saltspoonful	¼ teaspoon
Dessertspoonful	2 teaspoons
Teacupful	¾ cup
Coffeecupful	1 cup
Kitchencupful	1 cup
Tumblerful	½ pint
Wineglassful	4 tablespoons
Fluid dram	1 teaspoon
Dash	1/8 teaspoon
Gill	½ cup
Pound of milk	1 pint
Pound of eggs	1 dozen medium eggs
	9 large eggs

Few people realize that George Washington (1732-1799) was a man who was formally taught school only to the - elementary level. Yet he went on to become Commander in-Chief of the Continental Army in 1775. This great American also served as Chairman of the Constitutional

Convention. He later served his country as its first President from 1789 to 1797. Washington *"without making ostentatious professions of religion, was a sincere believer in the Christian faith, and a truly devout man,"* according to John Marshall, Chief Justice of the United States Supreme Court. Marshall had fought with General Washington at Valley Forge during the War for Independence. When first leaving home to serve his country as a young man, Washington recorded these parting words of his mother, Mary: *"Remember that God is our only sure trust. To Him, I commend you. ... My son, neglect not the duty of secret prayer."*

A special treat to make for Christmas would be this pudding topped with a foam sauce. It's truly a historical gem in that it was often enjoyed by George and Martha Washington over the Yuletide season. Here's how it was made for the Washington family:

10 crackers, crushed fine	1 tbls salt, heaping
4 cups milk	1 tbls nutmeg
8 eggs	½ tbls mace

2 cups sugar	1 tbls cloves
1 cup molasses	1 lemon rind,
1 cup brandy	grated
1 pound suet,	¼ cup citron
chopped fine	7 cups raisins

Stir the crushed crackers together with the milk in a kettle. Set aside and let stand overnight. In the morning, rub through a colander. Add the rest of the ingredients and blend thoroughly. Set on stove and bring to a boil. Let pudding boil for 5 hours. Serve with foam sauce as made below.

3 tbls butter	1 egg white,
1-1/2 cups powdered sugar	stiffly beaten
1 egg white	4 tbls sherry wine
3 tbls water, boiling	

Cream the butter and powdered sugar in a saucepan. Stir in the unbeaten egg white. Follow this by stirring in the stiffly beaten egg white. Whip together until fluffy. Add the sherry wine and boiling water. Set on stove and heat slightly. Stir continuously until sauce becomes frothy. Pour over pudding and serve immediately.

Yes, every recipe found in this unique book was a popular favorite throughout the Christmas holidays in our nation's long and colorful history. Many were coveted within a particular family and handed down from generation to generation. Others are historical gems, for they were the inventions of, or the favorites of, some notable family or individual from the past. Here they are being presented, for the first time, for America's families of today to have the fun and experience the thrill of cooking and baking. And lastly, to thankfully pass a blessing over before eating – be it for breakfast, lunch or dinner – on Christmas Day.

1

Flannel Cakes and Waffles for Christmas Breakfast

Sour Milk Griddle Cakes –
A Christmas Favorite of Mrs. Evarts

2 cups flour	1 tsp salt
½ tsp baking powder	2 cups sour milk
1-1/4 tsp baking soda	2 cups sour cream
1 egg, well beaten	

Sift together in a wooden mixing bowl the flour, baking powder, baking soda and salt. Beat in the sour milk, sour cream and beaten egg. Drop by large spoonfuls on hot, well-greased griddle. Cook until lightly browned on one side and then flip over. Brown on other side. Serve while hot with butter and maple syrup. Makes 16 nice griddle cakes.

** ** ** ** **

William Maxwell Evarts (1818-1901) of Boston was a widely known New York attorney who not only possessed a great legal mind but was also an unsurpassed orator. He was selected at the conclusion of the Civil War to serve as a member of the legal team hired by the government to prosecute former Confederate President Jefferson Davis. Prior to this, Evarts was sent to England by the Union government in 1863 and 1864. His task was an important one – to use his influence to forcibly persuade the British to stop building and equipping ships for the Confederate Navy. Evarts, a church going Christian, was also a member of the high powered legal team President Andrew Johnson used during his impeachment trial. Evarts alone, because of his phenomenal legal skills, is given most of the credit for keeping Johnson from being impeached and thrown out of office. Johnson duly rewarded him with an appointment as Attorney General of the United States where he served from 1867 and 1868. And he also served as Secretary of State under President Rutherford Hayes from 1877 to 1881.

French Potato Flannel Cakes –
A Patrick Henry Christmas Favorite

½ cup potato flour   5 eggs, well beaten

1 tsp baking powder   1 tbls water

2 tsp sugar   1 cup milk

Sift together in a wooden mixing bowl the potato flour, baking powder and sugar. Blend in the frothy beaten eggs, water and milk. Beat thoroughly to a creamy batter. Continue beating for a full 10 minutes more. Drop by large spoonfuls into large moderately hot, well-greased cast iron skillet. Lightly brown on both sides. When cooked, take from skillet and spread with apple or currant jelly. Roll up. Sprinkle with powdered sugar and a few drops of lemon juice. Serve while hot.

** ** ** ** **

Patrick Henry (1736-99), was a brilliant self-taught country lawyer from Colonial Virginia. This man was a renowned orator and statesman before and during the American Revolution. In fact, he was no doubt the most famous orator of the American Revolutionary period. According to Thomas Jefferson, Henry's dramatic and fiery speeches inspired those in the Colonies "far above all in maintaining the spirit of the Revolution." This great Christian patriot stated: ***"Bad men cannot make good citizens. It is impossible that a nation of infidels or idolaters should be a nation of free men. It is when a people forget God that tyrants forge their chains."***

Yes, Patrick Henry, was Commander-in-Chief of the Virginia Militia as well as a member of the Continental Congress for one session. Just before the Battle of Lexington and Concord in 1775, Henry proposed the immediate arming of the militia. This took place during Virginia's revolutionary convention in Richmond. He then delivered his most important speech of the revolution – and in all probability, *the* most famous speech *ever* given by any person during that period of our history: *"Gentlemen may cry peace, peace – but there is no peace. The war is actually begun ... Is life so dear, or peace so sweet, as to be purchased at the price of chains and slavery? Forbid it, Almighty God! I know not what course others may take, but as for me, give me liberty, or give me death!"* His proposal was promptly approved by the convention. Henry along with a number of others was also instrumental in establishing the Continental Army.

On the founding of our great Republic, this man unequivocally declared: *"It cannot be emphasized too strongly or too often that this great nation was founded not by religionists, but by Christians; not on religions, but on the Gospel of Jesus Christ."* Henry also holds the distinction, under the Constitution of 1776, of being the first man to be elected as Governor of Virginia.

Fried Flat Ham Cakes –
The Pelham's Christmas Morning Treat

¼ cup butter	¾ cup graham flour
¾ cup ham, cooked and chopped	1 cup flour
	3 tbls baking powder
1 egg, well beaten	1 cup milk

Put butter in a large wooden mixing bowl and beat to a creamy mixture. Blend in the chopped ham. Then add the frothy beaten egg and graham flour. Sift together in a separate bowl the flour and baking powder. Stir this into mixture in first bowl. Lastly blend in the milk. Beat thoroughly to a creamy batter. Drop by large spoonfuls into a hot, well-greased cast iron skillet. Lightly brown on both sides. Serve while hot with butter, salt and pepper.

** ** ** ** **

Lieutenant Colonel John Pelham (1838-63) was, according to General Robert E. Lee, *"gallant and courageous"* at Fredericksburg. Born in Alabama, this idealistic young soldier resigned his U.S. Army commission and left West Point in 1861 to offer his services to Jefferson Davis and the Confederate cause. Pelham, a dedicated Christian, was willing to fight and die for the cause in which he so strongly believed was – *"a Holy War with the unconditional blessing of God Almighty."* When this dashing 25-year old officer was killed at Kelley's Ford, it was reported that at least three lovely southern belles were known to have gone into mourning.

Oatmeal Flapjacks –
A Christmas Favorite of James Garfield

1 cup oatmeal,	2 tsp salt
cooked to mush	2 tbls sugar
2 cups milk	1-1/2 tbls baking powder
1 egg, well beaten	1 cup flour
3 tbls bacon grease	

Put oatmeal in large wooden mixing bowl. Blend in the milk, frothy beaten egg, salt and sugar. Sift together in a separate bowl the baking powder and flour. Stir this into the first mixture. Lastly blend in the bacon grease. Beat everything thoroughly to a creamy batter. Drop by large spoonfuls into hot, well-greased cast iron skillet. Lightly brown on both sides. Serve while hot with butter and syrup or sugar.

** ** ** ** **

James Abram Garfield (1831-81) pulled himself up by his bootstraps from a poor childhood and became a lay preacher, later a Union General during the War Between the States and finally the President of the United States. This remarkable Christian individualist led brigades at Shiloh, Middle Creek and Pound Gap and was General William Rosecrans Chief-of Staff in the Chickamauga Campaign. Garfield especially distinguished himself at Chickamauga in September of 1863. His horse was shot out from under him, yet he went on to heroically deliver a message that ultimately saved the Army of the Cumberland from a disastrous defeat. This brought him a well deserved promotion to Major General. Born in a crude log cabin on a frontier farm in Ohio, he had to borrow money to attend Williams College in Williamstown, Massachusetts. A brilliant student, Garfield graduated with honors in 1856. And at the age of only 26, he became president of Hiram College, a school founded by the Disciples of Christ. When the Civil War broke out, Garfield was elected lieutenant colonel of a company of Hiram College students attached to the 42nd Ohio Volunteers. He courageously led a brigade against Confederate troops and drove them out of Eastern Kentucky. As a result of this, Garfield was commissioned at the age of 30 as a Brigadier General.

Corn Meal Pancakes –
As Eaten by Henry Knox as a Boy

1 cup flour	2 tsp salt
1 cup corn meal	2 cups milk
3 tsp baking powder	3 eggs, well beaten

1 tbls molasses

Sift together in a wooden mixing bowl the flour, corn meal, baking powder and salt. In a separate bowl whip together the milk and frothy beaten eggs. Combine the two mixtures and stir well. Lastly blend in the molasses. Beat thoroughly to a creamy batter. Drop by large spoonfuls into a hot, well-greased cast iron skillet. Lightly brown on both sides. Serve while hot with butter and syrup or sugar. Note: Mrs. Knox sometimes substituted honey for molasses in this recipe.

** ** ** ** **

Henry Knox (1750-1806) was an outstanding military leader during the American War for Independence. This devout Christian was one of George Washington's most trusted advisors. Born and raised in Boston of Scot-Irish heritage, Knox was active early on in the Revolutionary movement with his involvement in the Boston Militia. He fought heroically at Bunker Hill and in almost every other major battle of the war. Knox was promoted to the rank of Major General after the British defeat at Yorktown. Washington appointed his long-time friend to be the first United States Secretary of War under the new *Constitution*.

Breakfast Spice Griddle Cakes –
A Specialty Made by Mary Surratt

1 egg	3 cups flour
2 cups sour milk	1 tsp baking soda
1 tbls sugar	½ tsp salt
¼ tsp nutmeg	1 tbls butter, melted

Cinnamon to suit

Beat egg in a wooden mixing bowl and then blend in the sour milk, sugar and nutmeg. Sift together in a separate bowl the flour, baking soda and salt. Stir these dry ingredients into the first bowl. Lastly add the melted butter. Mix until everything is thoroughly blended. Cook on a hot, well-greased griddle in cakes the size of a breakfast plate or saucer. Lightly brown on both sides. When done, pile several on top of one another on a warm plate. Spread each layer liberally with butter, syrup and a sprinkling of cinnamon. To serve, cut through whole pile, pie-fashion. Makes 8 generous servings.

** ** ** ** **

Mary Surratt's son John was a Confederate spy during the early years of the Civil War. Mary was known to be a decent, Godly woman, who simply ran a boarding house in Washington where John Wilkes Booth and his fellow conspirators met and planned the assassination of President Abraham Lincoln. Nevertheless, due to the political atmosphere of the times, she was arrested as part of the conspiracy. A military court convicted this woman and she was hanged on July 7, 1865, although there was really no evidence that she had any involvement with Booth and the others. Lincoln's Secretary of War Edwin Stanton offered a reward of $25,000 for the capture of conspirators John Surratt and David E. Herold. But John escaped his pursuers and fled to Canada after Lincoln's assassination. He finally returned to America in 1867 and was tried but not convicted as his trial resulted in a hung jury.

Sour Cream Waffles –
A Morris Family Breakfast Treat

1 cup flour	3 tbls butter, melted
¾ tsp baking powder	1 egg yolk, beaten
¼ tsp baking soda	1 cup sour cream, thick
¾ tsp salt	¼ cup milk
1 egg white, well beaten	

Sift together in a wooden mixing bowl the flour, baking powder, baking soda and salt. In a separate bowl, stir together the melted butter and beaten egg yolk. Blend in the sour cream and milk. Stir this into bowl of dry ingredients. Mix together just enough to moisten everything well. Lastly, carefully fold in the stiffly beaten egg white. Put batter in a pitcher and pour correct amount onto hot, well-greased waffle iron. Close top and cook until done. Serve while hot with butter and syrup. Makes 4 large waffles.

** ** ** ** **

Gouverneur Morris (1752-1816) was a noted delegate to the Constitutional Convention from Philadelphia. He wrote the final draft of the *Constitution* and was the originator of the phrase, *"We the people of the United States."* This great man was known to be a superb speaker and writer, using his many talents in the debates that shaped this great document. He spoke 173 times during the debates, more than any other delegate did. Gouverneur Morris is the man who served under Robert Morris and managed the finances for the Congress. He is responsible for coming up with the idea of the dollar being used as the basis of American money. Morris was also a highly respected member of the Continental Congress as well as a diplomat, statesman and financier. He once wrote: *"Religion is the only solid basis of good morals; therefore education should teach the precepts of religion, and the duties of man toward God."*

2

Special Holiday Soups, Salads and Chowders of Long Ago

Celery Soup –
As Made for Gunning Bedford

4 tbls butter, melted	1 tsp onion, grated
4 tbls flour	2 cups milk
Pinch of paprika	1 cup celery, cooked
Pinch of pepper	and diced
1-1/2 tsp salt	2 cups celery water

Blend in a cast iron kettle the melted butter, flour, paprika, pepper, salt and grated onion. Let simmer 3 minutes and then stir in milk. Let simmer while constantly stirring until thickened. Then add celery and celery water. Continue to let mixture simmer for 35 minutes. Pour into bowls and serve while hot. Makes enough soup to feed 4 people.

** ** ** ** **

Gunning Bedford (1747-1812) is a man often forgotten with the passage of time, but he was an instrumental force in American history. This man was a Delaware delegate to the Constitutional Convention and a signer of our *Constitution*. While attending Princeton, he and James Madison were roommates. And he was one of many great Americans who studied under John Witherspoon, the country's leading legal scholar and theologian of the period. Bedford, a devout Christian, believed that the *Bible* was *"given by divine inspiration,"* and he openly professed faith *"in God the Father, and in Jesus Christ, His only Son."*

Vegetable Soup –

As Served to Andrew Jackson

¼ cup butter	5 cups water, boiling
½ cup turnips, diced	½ cup cabbage, shredded
½ cup onions, diced	¼ tsp celery salt
½ cup carrots, diced	1 cup potatoes, diced
½ cup tomatoes, diced	Salt to suit taste
Pepper to suit taste	

Put butter in cast iron kettle and melt. Add diced turnips, onions, and carrots. Simmer and stir until vegetables are nicely browned. Then stir in diced tomatoes, boiling water, shredded cabbage, celery salt and diced potatoes. Cover kettle and let simmer until vegetables are tender. Stir every few minutes. Add salt and pepper to taste. Serve while hot. Makes 8 nice servings.

** ** ** ** **

Andrew Jackson (1767-1845) was the 7th President of the United States who served his country in this position from 1829 to 1837. This man grew to greatness after a turbulent boyhood as an orphan. He became a noted frontiersman who thoroughly enjoyed cock fighting and dueling. A devout Christian, Jackson wrote his son, Andrew Jr., a letter on September 11, 1834, in which he said: *"I nightly offer up my prayers to the throne of grace for the health and safety of you all, and that we ought all to rely with confidence on the promises of our dear Redeemer, and give Him our hearts. This is all he requires and all that we can do, and if we sincerely do this, we are sure of salvation through his atonement."*

Chicken Corn Meal Soup –
Andrew Johnson's Christmas Favorite

6 cups chicken broth   1 cup corn meal

½ cup onion, diced   1 cup chicken, cooked

1 cup potatoes, diced   and diced

1 garlic clove, minced   Salt to suit taste

Pepper to suit taste

Put chicken broth in small kettle and bring to a boil. Stir in diced onions, diced potatoes and minced garlic. Cover and let simmer until vegetables are tender. Then slowly sift in the corn meal while constantly stirring. Now add diced chicken. Salt and pepper to taste. Cover again and allow to simmer for another 10 minutes. Take from stove and serve while hot. Makes enough soup to feed 10 people.

** ** ** ** **

Andrew Johnson (1805-75), born in abject poverty in Raleigh, North Carolina, rose to serve as Abraham Lincoln's Vice-President. At this point in his career and loyal to the Union, he forthrightly denounced the secessionists: *"I would have them arrested and tried for treason, and, if convicted, by the eternal God, they should suffer the penalty of the law at the hands of the executioner."* He then assumed the Presidency when Lincoln was assassinated by John Wilkes Booth. Johnson, a Christian, tried to follow Lincoln's moderate reconstruction plan for the defeated South. He issued a proclamation of amnesty and pardoned those who had been involved in the secession. His moderate reconstruction policies were thwarted by hostile Radical Republicans in Congress who overrode a Presidential veto and rammed through a series of harsh Reconstruction Acts in the spring of 1867. Johnson was a decent man who once proclaimed: *"I do believe in Almighty God! I also believe in the Bible.*

Herring Salad –
Alexander Hamilton Enjoyed This One

4 lettuce leaves, large	2 small beets, diced
2 large salted herrings, raw	6 eggs, hard boiled
	6 small pickled onions
8 potatoes, boiled and diced	6 small gherkins
2 sour apples, diced	2 tbls olive oil
	3 tbls cider vinegar

Lay lettuce leaves in the bottom of a salad bowl. Skin and bone the herring. Cut into small pieces and sprinkle evenly on lettuce leaves. Now put in the diced potatoes, sour apples and beets. Garnish with slices of hard boiled eggs, pickled onions and gherkins. Dress with mixture of olive oil and cider vinegar.

** ** ** ** **

Alexander Hamilton (1757-1804) was born in the West Indies and didn't come to the Colonies until 1772. Yet, he immediately joined in the fight for American independence and became one of the Republic's brightest stars. Hamilton was one of General George Washington's closest friends and most trusted advisors during the Revolutionary War. He later became Washington's Secretary of the Treasury. A brilliant essayist, Hamilton's writings strongly urged the ratification of the *Constitution*. These essays were later published as **The Federalist**, which also contained important contributions from John Jay and James Madison as well. Hamilton's life was ended when he was mortally wounded in a duel with Aaron Burr, former Vice-President under Thomas Jefferson. His dying words were: *"I have a tender reliance on the mercy of the Almighty, through the merits of the Lord Jesus Christ. I am a sinner. I look to Him for mercy; pray for me."*

Ox Tail Soup –
As Enjoyed by William Floyd

1 Ox tail	1 bay leave
1 tbls butter	½ cup tomatoes,
1 large onion, diced	chopped
3 pints beef stock	1 cup red wine
1 carrot, sliced thin	1 tbls meat sauce
1 celery stalk, sliced thin	6 peppercorns,
1 sprig thyme	crushed
2 sprigs parsley	Salt to suit taste

Wash ox tail carefully and split into small pieces. Melt butter in a large kettle and toss in ox tail pieces. When beginning to brown, add diced onion. Fry until onion is a deep golden color. Then pour in beef stock, sliced carrot and celery. Stir well. Tie the thyme, parsley and bay leaf securely together and toss into kettle. Add tomatoes and red wine. Season with meat sauce, crushed peppercorns and salt. Let mixture boil up once. Then cover and put in oven to roast at 275 degrees for 8 hours. Take out and remove thyme, parsley and bay leaf. Separate meat from ox tail bones and give bones to the dogs. Serve a little of the meat in each bowl of soup as it is served.

** ** ** ** **

William Floyd (1734-1821) of New York was another often forgotten man in American history. He was a wealthy landowner-farmer who signed the *Declaration of Independence* and ultimately paid dearly for his bravery. In retaliation, British troops were ordered to destroy this Christian patriot's estate, methodically ravage his land and plunder his belongings. His wife and family were forced to flee from Long Island Sound to a 7-year exile in Connecticut. There she passed away in 1781, never again able to return to their home place. When Floyd and his children finally returned in 1783, his home which had been used by the British as a barracks, had been badly damaged. All the timber had been stripped from his land, fences destroyed and fields burned. Yes, William Floyd paid a high price for his unwavering stand for liberty and freedom. Yet he stood tall and never regretted what he had so freely given for the great American cause.

Clam or Fish Chowder –

A Christmas Favorite of General Kearney

¼ pound salt pork, diced	Salt to suit taste
2 medium onions	Pepper to suit taste
6 large potatoes	1 quart clams
1 cup fresh corn	6 cups milk
1 cup parsnips, cut up	2 tbls butter, melted
1 tbls flour	

Put diced pieces of salt pork in kettle and fry until nicely browned. Meanwhile slice onions. Also slice potatoes and quarter the slices. Add these to kettle with corn and cut up parsnips. Season with salt and pepper to taste. Cover mixture with boiling water. Bring to a boil and then let simmer until potato slices and parsnips are tender. Then stir in clams and milk. Bring to a boil. Meanwhile blend the melted butter and flour. Add this to mixture in kettle. Allow to cook 5 minutes more. Serve while hot with crisp crackers. *Note: Baked fish, shredded salmon and other kinds of fish were often substituted in place of clams by the Kearney family.*

** ** ** ** **

Union General Winfield Scott called Philip Kearney (1814-62) ***"The bravest and most perfect soldier"*** he had ever known. General Kearney, known to be a devout, *Bible* believing Christian, had an outstanding record during the Civil War. He was a dashing, one-armed cavalry officer whose men always rode distinctive dapple-gray horses into battle. Kearney was killed at Chantilly in September of 1862. Met by Confederate troops in the midst of a furious battle, Kearney was asked to surrender. He refused. He was shot in the back as he rode away. This fearless warrior fell from his horse and was dead in an instant. He had died in service to his country – just as he had wanted to do.

Oyster Soup –
As Served to Thomas Nelson

3 tbls butter	1-1/2 tsp salt
2 tbls flour	¼ tsp pepper
3 cups milk	1 tbls onion, grated
1 cup cream	1 quart oysters

Melt the butter in a small kettle. Then stir in flour and blend thoroughly. Slowly add the milk while constantly stirring. Next add the cream, salt, pepper and grated onion. Keep mixture simmering over low heat. Put oysters in a separate kettle and bring to boil in their own liquor (juice). Let them cook for about 5 minutes or until edges curl. Then strain off liquid and add oysters to kettle with milk mixture. Keep simmering for about 5 more minutes but do not allow to boil. Pour into bowls and serve immediately.

** ** ** ** **

Thomas Nelson, Jr. (1738-89), born in Yorktown, Virginia, was yet another heroic signer of the *Declaration of Independence*. As a brigadier general, he commanded the 3,000 member Virginia Militia. While attending a convention in Williamsburg in May of 1776, Nelson, introduced a resolution calling for independence. His proposal was approved. This great American patriot spent much of his time soliciting money from wealthy plantation owners to help support the Revolutionary War effort. He promised to personally repay their loans should the government fail to do so. He also devoted much of his efforts to obtaining weapons, munitions and supplies for the militia. Nelson, a dedicated Christian, declared: *"I call to God to witness that if any British troops are landed in the County of York ... I will wait no orders, but will summon the militia and drive the invaders into the sea."* In 1781, this unselfish patriot personally ordered the destruction of his own mansion when he discovered it had been taken over by the British invaders and was being used as their headquarters. Nelson died in abject poverty as an end result of his numerous sacrifices for the great American cause in which he so fervently believed.

3

Vegetable Dishes from Christmas Days Gone By

Scalloped Corn Dish –
The Ellery's Christmas Favorite

1-1/2 cups milk	½ tsp salt
¼ cup butter, melted	1 tbls sugar
¼ cup flour	1 cup bread crumbs
1 pint fresh corn	2 tbls cream

Heat milk in small kettle. Mix melted butter and flour together. Add this to hot milk while constantly stirring. Then put corn in the kettle. Stir in salt and sugar. Let come to a boil and immediately turn out into a baking pan. Moisten bread crumbs slightly with the cream. Cover the top of mixture in baking pan with this. Bake at 350 degrees for 15 to 20 minutes.

** ** ** ** **

William Ellery (1727-1820) of Rhode Island was a member of the Continental Congress andanother brave signer of the *Declaration of Independence*. He deliberately stood close to the table where each man came forth to affix his signature to the great document. This unwavering Christian hero said that he wanted ***"to see how they all looked as they signed what might be their death warrants."*** He reported that he observed "undaunted resolution" on every man's face as they boldly penned their names on the historic document. We must not forget that each of these men would have been hanged had the British been victorious and defeated the Colonists in the War for American Independence. During the British 3 year occupation of Newport, Rhode Island, Ellery personally suffered great losses when his home and property were destroyed in 1778. But he bore all this with a quiet cheerfulness as a sacrifice for the public good.

Kidney Beans in Bacon Sauce –
A Grant Christmas Family Favorite

1-1/2 cups kidney beans, dry	1 cup onion, chopped fine
3 cups water	1-1/2 tsp salt
3 slices bacon	Pinch of pepper

Wash kidney beans thoroughly. Put in kettle with the water and let soak overnight. In the morning, cook beans until tender in the same water in which they were soaked. Meanwhile, fry bacon in a cast iron skillet until nice and crispy. Break up bacon into small pieces. Add onions. Sauté until lightly browned. Pour mixture over kidney beans, Add salt and pepper. Serve while steaming hot. Makes enough to feed 5 people.

** ** ** ** **

Ulysses Simpson Grant (1822-85) was a prominent Union General during the Civil War and 18th President of the United States from 1869 to 1877. He was known to be a brilliant military tactician and a man with all the qualities of a great military leader. Grant was a relentless warrior, constantly hammering away at the enemy. He was ever persistent, a man of quiet determination and calm resolution. Grant, a devout Christian, offered this comment to the editor of the **Sunday School Times** in Philadelphia: *"My advice to Sunday schools, no matter what their denomination, is: Hold fast to the Bible as the sheet anchor of your liberties; write its precepts in your hearts, and practice them in your lives. To the influence of this Book are we indebted for all the progress made in true civilization, and to this must we look as our guide in the future. 'Righteousness exalteth a nation; but sin is a reproach to any people'"*

Sweet and Sour Cabbage –
Richard Henry Lee's Favorite

1 cup water	2 tbls flour
3 cups cabbage,	1/3 cup vinegar
coarsely shredded	½ tsp salt
4 slices bacon	Pinch of pepper
2 tbls maple sugar	2 tbls onion, minced

Put water and cabbage in kettle and bring to boil. Let simmer 7 minutes. Meanwhile put bacon in cast iron skillet and fry until nice and crisp. Remove bacon, chop in small pieces, and set aside. Add maple sugar and flour to bacon grease in skillet. Blend thoroughly. Add ½ cup water, vinegar, salt and pepper. Let simmer while stirring constantly until mixture thickens. Then stir in bacon pieces and minced onion. Garnish with additional fried bacon slices if desired. Makes enough to feed 5 people.

** ** ** ** **

Richard Henry Lee (1732-94) a Virginian, was a direct descendant of early settlers of the Colony. This great American patriot was a man of strong Christian convictions. He was one of the early heroes in the Colonies to openly come out in favor of independence. Lee was a delegate to both the First and Second Continental Congress. He was the man who introduced the resolution for independence before the Continental Congress on July 2, 1776. And he also was the man who proposed the most important 10th Amendment to the *Constitution*, which specifically limited the power of the Federal Government. It reads as follows: ***"Rights reserved to the States and the People. The powers not delegated to the United States by the Constitution, nor prohibited by it to the States, are reserved to the States respectively, or to the people."***

Stuffed Sweet Potatoes –
As Enjoyed by John Hancock

Sweet potatoes, oval   Salt to suit taste

Cream to suit   Pepper to suit taste

Maple sugar to suit

Select a number of medium-sized, smooth skinned, slender sweet potatoes. Bake them at 425 degrees until tender. Be careful to not crisp the skins. When done, slice each sweet potato lengthwise. Carefully scoop out the soft pulp and put in a wooden mixing bowl. Be sure not to break potato skins when doing this. Set the sweet potato skins aside. Mash the hot pulp and add enough cream to make mixture soft like mashed potatoes. Stir in ¼ teaspoon salt and 1/8 teaspoon pepper for every cup of the sweet potato mixture in the bowl. Fill potato shells with this mixture. Round the surface so it looks like the shape of the original sweet potato. Sprinkle maple sugar over the top of each and bake at 425 degrees for 10 minutes.

** ** ** ** **

John Hancock (1737-93) was the first man to boldly step forward and affix his signature to the *Declaration of Independence*. He exclaimed loudly enough for everyone in attendance to hear: *"There! His Majesty can now read my name without spectacles, and can now double his reward of 500 pounds for my head. That is my defiance!"* He gained a great deal of lasting fame for uttering those words and for penning the largest name on the document. This man served as the President of the Second Continental Congress and he later became the first elected Governor of Massachusetts. Hancock's final great service to his nation was to have the honor of presiding over the Massachusetts convention when it ratified the *Constitution*. On November 8, 1783, Hancock, a Christian, issued a special proclamation to celebrate the victorious end of the War for American Independence. It said in part: *" ... the Citizens of these United States have every Reason for Praise and Gratitude to the God of their salvation."*

Savory Country Lentils –
As Made for General Sherman

1-1/2 cups dry lentils	¼ cup celery, diced
2-1/2 tsp salt	1-1/2 tbls flour
½ pound salt pork, diced	3 tbls vinegar
½ cup onions, minced	½ cup water, hot

Pinch of pepper

Wash and carefully pick over lentils. Put in kettle with 6 cups cold water. Let Soak overnight. In the morning, drain. Add 4-1/2 cups cold water with 1-1/2 teaspoons salt. Cover kettle and bring to boil. Let simmer until lentils are tender. Drain and set aside. Fry the diced salt pork in cast iron skillet. When salt pork pieces are crisp and browned nicely, add minced onions and diced celery. Slowly fry 5 minutes more. Stir in flour and blend everything thoroughly. Then add vinegar, hot water, previously cooked lentils, 1 teaspoon salt and the pepper. Let simmer until mixture thickens. Makes enough to feed 6 people.

** ** ** ** **

William Tecumseh Sherman (1820-91), son of an Ohio Supreme Court Justice, led his Union troops to victory in Charleston, South Carolina, on February 18, 1865. He soundly thrashed Confederate General Beauregard and occupied the beautiful city. Sherman was without doubt one of the greatest of all Union commanders in the Civil War. As he started his now famous "March to the Sea" on November 15, 1864, he told General Grant: *"I can make Georgia howl."* He then proceeded to march his 60,000-man army through the interior of Georgia, cutting a 60-mile swath of indescribable devastation and destruction. Orphaned at the age of 9, this man was raised by a wealthy friend of his father. He went on to graduate near the top of his class at West Point in 1840. Brought up in a Christian centered family, Sherman was taught to never doubt the infallibility of the Bible, or as he was to say, *"Jesus Christ, my Saviour."*

Special Parsnip Dishes –
As Prepared by Mrs. Mary Randolph

Parsnips are always best if dug up just after a hard freeze. Wash, peel, and cut up lengthwise. Bring them to a quick boil in a little water, then simmer for about 20 minutes, or until tender.

Here's how Mrs. Randolph wrote one of her original recipes in her 1824 book, **The Virginia Housewife**: *"PARSPIPS, Are to be cooked just in the same manner as carrots; they require more or less time, according to their size; therefore match them in size, and you must try them by thrusting a fork into them as they are in the water; when this goes easily through, they are done enough: boil them from an hour to two hours, according to their size and freshness. Parsnips are sometimes sent up mashed in the same way as turnips."*

To Serve as Cooked: Simply add melted butter to the cooked parsnips. Or if desired, add ¼ cup cream to them. Better yet, stir 2 tablespoons flour through the boiled parsnips, add 1 cup milk, and simmer until it thickens.

To Pan Fry Parsnips: Heat meat drippings or butter in skillet. Brown a batch of parsnips that have been previously cooked. Salt and pepper to suit and serve while hot.

Note: If you remove the core before cooking, or after cooking but before pan frying or creaming, the flavor will be greatly improved. One pound of parsnips will feed 3 people.

** ** ** ** **

39

In 1860, **The Virginia Housewife** was published in Philadelphia by the E. H. Butler & Company. Mistress Mary Randolph, the author, wrote of housewives: *"She must begin the day with an early breakfast, requiring each person to be in readiness to take their seats when the muffins, buckwheat cakes, etc., are placed on the table. ... No work can be done until breakfast is finished."* Her book was initially published in 1824 and is credited with being the first cook book ever published in the South. Randolph, a devout Christian lady, declared that most of her recipes were *"written from memory, where they were impressed by long continued practice."*

Baked Lima Beans –

As Made for the Farragut Family

1-1/2 cups lima beans, dried	1 tbls salt
	¼ tsp dry mustard
3 cups cold water	1 tbls dark molasses
½ pound salt pork, diced	1 tbls brown sugar

Pick over and carefully wash the lima beans. Put in kettle and cover with cold water. Let soak overnight. In the morning, add diced salt pork. Bring to a quick boil and then let simmer until lima beans are soft. Drain off liquid and set aside. Place beans in large buttered baking pan. Then combine in a small mixing bowl the salt, dry mustard, dark molasses, brown sugar and enough bean liquid to make 1 cup. If not enough liquid is left, add water. Pour over lima beans in baking pan and cover. Bake at 350 degrees for 1-1/2 hours. Serve while hot. Makes enough to feed 6 people.

** ** ** ** **

David Glasgow Farragut (1801-70) became the first Admiral in the United States Navy during the Civil War. On August 5, 1864, he destroyed the Confederate fleet in Mobile Bay. He is best remembered in history for his famous declaration: *"Damn the torpedoes. Full steam ahead!"* Admiral Farragut's son, Loyall, wrote that his father, a Christian, had once told him: *"He never felt so near his Master as he did when in a storm, knowing that on his skill depended the safety of so many lives."*

4

Old-Fashioned Christmas Stews, Pot Pies and Casseroles

Chuck Roast Goulash –
A Paul Revere Family Favorite

2 cups noodles

2 pounds chuck roast	1 green pepper, chopped
Flour to suit	1 medium onion, diced
1 cup salt pork, diced	2 cups carrots, diced
2 cups tomatoes,	2 tbls parsley, minced
crushed	4 whole cloves
½ cup celery, diced	Salt to suit taste

Pepper to suit taste

Put noodles in kettle, cook in boiling salted water, and set aside to be used later. Cut chuck roast into 1-inch cubes and roll in flour. Combine the beef cubes with diced salt pork in a large, well-greased kettle and fry until everything is nicely browned. Stir constantly so as not to burn. Add sufficient water to prevent sticking. Cover and let simmer until meat is tender. Then add to this the crushed tomatoes, diced celery, chopped green pepper, diced onion, diced carrots, minced parsley and whole cloves. Add salt and pepper to suit taste. Add enough water to cover everything in kettle. Let simmer until vegetables are tender. Now put noodles on plates. Spoon mixture over the noodles and serve immediately..

** ** ** ** **

Paul Revere (1734-1818), silversmith, engraver, soldier and patriot, started his historic ride to Lexington at 10 p.m. on April 15, 1775. His task was to rouse the leader of the minutemen at Medford and alert every household along his route of the impending British attack. One of his main missions was to warn John Hancock and Samuel Adams of the approaching danger, and to persuade them to seek a safer place to hide. These two men were considered by the British to be the rebel chiefs of the Independence movement. And they believed that if they were able to capture them it would break its back. Long before his memorable ride, Revere made numerous engravings designed to stir up public wrath against British oppression in the Colonies. This devout *Bible* believing Christian patriot went on to serve as a Lieutenant Colonel in the Revolutionary War and he later opened the first copper rolling mill in North America in 1801.

Pork Chop Stew –

A Custer Christmas Favorite

6 lean pork chops	1 green pepper, cut
6 tbls rice, uncooked	in strips
1 large onion, sliced	Salt to suit
2 tomatoes, sliced	Pepper to suit
3 cups hot water	

Put pork chops in large cast iron skillet and sear on both sides. Remove chops from skillet and place in baking pan. On each pork chop place 1 tablespoon uncooked rice, an onion slice, a slice of tomato and 2 strips of green pepper. Sprinkle all over chops with salt and pepper. Lastly add the hot water and cover. Bake at 350 degrees for 3 to 4 hours.

** ** ** ** **

George Armstrong Custer (1839-76) was a hell-bent for leather cavalry rider -- a man who had been brought up in a family with strong Christian convictions. He was a tall and handsome fellow – a dashing figure with a head full of blond flowing curly hair. Custer was undeniably courageous, and not just a little on the flamboyant side. He is best remembered for his famous "Last Stand" against Sitting Bull and his Sioux warriors on June 22, 1876, at the Battle of Little Big Horn. Little do most people realize that this man was an 1861 West Point graduate who had fought with great distinction in many Civil War battles. Never without a *Bible* in his pack, Custer saw action at Bull Run, Gettysburg, Richmond, Winchester, Fisher's Hill, Cedar Creek, Five Forks and Appomattox. More than 10,000 Confederate prisoners had been captured by the men under his command.

Corn and Celery Casserole –
A Meade Family Christmas Dish

2 tbls butter,	¾ tsp salt
1 cup celery, chopped	Dash of pepper
½ cup green pepper, chopped	½ cup bread crumbs, buttered
2 cups corn	3 slices bacon, fried crisp
½ cup milk	

Melt butter in a cast iron skillet. Add chopped celery and green pepper. Sauté for about 10 minutes until nicely browned. Stir in the corn, milk, salt and pepper. Dump everything into buttered baking pan or casserole dish. Sprinkle over top with soft buttered bread crumbs. Crumble crisp bacon slices and sprinkle these on top of bread crumbs. Bake at 350 degrees for 35 minutes. Serve while hot.

** ** ** ** **

Union General George Gordon Meade (1815-72) was the man who was most instrumental in the defeat of General Robert E. Lee at Gettysburg in July of 1863. The victory over Lee is believed to have been the one most important loss of the Civil War. As General Meade lay on his death bed, his son, Colonel George Meade wrote: *"He looked to the Saviour, who was the only one in Heaven or earth who could help him. He asked for the Holy Communion, and by the Lord's table gathered manna for the last journey. The words of penitence and the look of faith were blended with his dying prayers."*

Rabbit Pot Pie –

A Favorite of the Sampson Family

2 young rabbits	1 garlic clove, minced
1 onion, sliced thin	Salt to suit taste
2 slices bacon, cut in	Pepper to suit taste
small pieces	Flour as required

Skin and clean (dress) the rabbits. Wash thoroughly. Cut into pieces suitable for serving. Put pieces of rabbit in a kettle and cover with boiling water. Add onion slices, bacon pieces, minced garlic, salt and pepper. Cover kettle tightly and let simmer until meat is tender. Now take pieces of rabbit from kettle and lay in a baking pan. Thicken broth in kettle with flour. Use about 2 tablespoons flour for each cup of broth. When suitably thickened, pour this gravy over rabbit pieces in baking pan and set aside momentarily.

Now prepare some of Deborah Sampson's *Special Rich Biscuit Dough* as follows:

2 cups flour	4 tbls butter
4 tbls baking powder	1 egg
½ tsp salt	½ cup milk

Sift together in a wooden mixing bowl the flour, baking powder and salt. Work the butter in with a fork. Beat the egg and then stir in the milk. Blend this in with the dry ingredients in the mixing bowl. Turn dough out onto a lightly floured board and roll or pat out to a sheet ¼ inch thick. Cut slits to allow steam to escape. Place this sheet of dough over rabbit mixture in baking pan. Bake at 475 degrees for about 12 minutes. Makes 8 nice servings.

** ** ** ** **

Deborah Sampson (1760-1827) was the first American woman who is known to have impersonated a man during the Revolutionary War in order to fight for her country. Yes, this 5'-7" woman bravely joined the Continental Army's Massachusetts Regiment under the name of Robert Shurtleff on May 20, 1782. Although a devout Christian, Deborah was excommunicated from the First Baptist Church of Middleborough, Massachusetts, because of rumors circulating that she was *"dressing in man's clothing and enlisting as a soldier in the army."* Deborah was wounded in one of her legs at Tarrytown but took care of herself so no one could discover that she was a woman in disguise. However, she was later hospitalized in Philadelphia with a fever and a doctor uncovered her secret. He quietly made arrangements for her to be honorably discharged on October 25, 1783, by General Henry Knox. Deborah then returned home, married Benjamin Gannett, bore him three children and taught school. A special Act of Congress awarded her children compensation *"for the relief of the heirs of Deborah Gannett, a soldier of the Revolution."*

50

Beef Heart Stew –

As Enjoyed on by John Morton

4 pounds of beef heart	1 garlic clove, minced
3 tbls carrot, cubed	2 tbls flour
3 tbls onion, grated	2 tbls butter, melted
2 stalks celery, chopped	1 tbls cider vinegar

½ tsp salt

Wash the beef heart in cold water. Carefully remove all veins and tough fibers. Cut heart up into small pieces and put in kettle. Cover with water and let sit 20 minutes. Drain. Now add enough boiling water to cover meat. Put in the cubed carrots, grated onion, chopped celery and minced garlic. Cover and gently simmer for 3 to 4 hours. Stir every so often. Add a little more water if required so as not to burn. Lastly, blend flour and melted butter. Add this to the hot stew along with the cider vinegar and salt. Stir until stew thickens. Serve over steamed rice. Makes enough to feed 6 people.

** ** ** ** **

John Morton (1725-1777) was another brave signer of the *Declaration of Independence* who paid dearly for his patriotism and his dedication to freedom and liberty. A delegate to the Continental Congress and close friend of Benjamin Franklin, he was one of the nine signers from Pennsylvania. Morton cast the decisive ballot that swung Pennsylvania over to a "yes" vote for independence. He became ill and died at the age of 51 in the spring of 1777, within a year of signing the *Declaration of Independence*. This staunch *Bible* believing Christian was rejected by his family and friends for his heroic deed. Morton spoke these final words from his death bed: ***"Tell them that they will live to see the hour when they shall acknowledge it [the signing] to have been the most glorious service that I ever rendered to my country."*** Yes, even to the taking of his last breath, John Morton believed with all his heart that he had done the right thing. He never doubted, never wavered in his convictions.

Oyster Pot Pie –
Thomas Jefferson's Christmas Treat

First Make Pastry as Follows:

2 cups pastry flour	½ tsp salt
½ tsp baking powder	½ cup lard
5 to 6 tbls ice water	

Sift together in a wooden mixing bowl the pastry flour, baking powder and salt. Work in the lard with a fork or the finger tips until everything is crumbly. Then add ice water, a tablespoon at a time, until mixture is moist enough to hold together as a dough. Knead it lightly until it is smooth. Divide dough in half and put on lightly floured board. Roll out one ball of dough to a 1/8 inch thick sheet. Fit into pie pan. Trim the edges even with edges of pan. Roll out second dough ball and place this crust on baking sheet. Cut to fit as top crust on pot pie. Bake both together at 475 for about 10 minutes or until crusts are a delicate brown. Then set them both aside momentarily while making the filling.

Make Filling as Follows:

1 quart oysters	2 tbls flour
½ tsp mace	2 tbls butter
1 glass white wine	2 egg yolks, well beaten
1 lemon, juice only	Salt to suit taste
1 cup cream	Pepper to suit taste

Take the oysters and pour off the juice into small kettle. Add the mace, white wine and lemon juice. Bring to boil. Stir in cream. Blend flour and butter together. Add this to mixture in kettle and stir. When gravy begins to thicken nicely, stir in beaten egg yolks. Lastly drop in the oysters. Salt and pepper to suit taste. Bring to a boil. Immediately pour into pie pan with prepared pastry crust. Carefully lay the pre-prepared upper crust on top and serve while piping hot.

** ** ** ** **

Thomas Jefferson (1743-1826) was America's first Secretary of State and the second Vice-President. He was also the 3rd President of the United States and served his country in this position from 1801 to 1809. Jefferson was among the most brilliant men of his time. He was a man of many talents -- an inventor, literary genius, statesman, architect, educator, diplomat and a man of limitless intellectual curiosity. His probing, wide-ranging mind delved into law, geology, botany, linguistics, art, music, food, agriculture, meteorology, etc. Uniquely enough, he died on July 4, the 50th anniversary of the signing of the *Declaration of Independence*, the magnificent document he had authored and signed. His death preceded that of another signer and dear friend, John Adams, by only a few hours. Was Thomas Jefferson a Christian? Let him answer this question: ***"I am a real Christian; that is to say, a disciple of the doctrines of Jesus. ... I am a Christian in the only sense in which He wished any one to be; sincerely attached to His doctrines in preference to all others. ... "***

Squirrel Stew –

A Read Christmas Family Favorite

3 Squirrels	6 ears corn
4 quarts water	6 potatoes, quartered
1 tbls salt	1 tsp pepper
½ pound salt pork, cut in 1 inch cubes	2 tsp sugar
	4 cups tomatoes
1 onion, minced	¼ pound butter
2 cups lima beans	1 tbls tapioca

Salt and pepper to suit taste

Skin and clean (dress) the squirrels. Wash thoroughly. Cut into pieces suitable for serving and set aside. Now put 4 quarts of water in a large kettle, add salt, and bring to a boil. When boiling, add cubed salt pork pieces, minced onion, lima beans, ears of corn, quartered potatoes, pepper and the pieces of squirrel. Cover kettle closely and let simmer 2 hours. Then add sugar and tomatoes. Simmer 1 more hour. Cut the butter to pieces the size of a walnut and roll in flour. Add chunks of butter to stew 10 minutes before it is taken from stove. Stir in tapioca to thicken gravy. Serve while hot in soup bowls. Add salt and pepper as desired to suit individual taste.

** ** ** ** **

George Read (1733-98) was a delegate from Delaware to the Constitutional Convention. A true American patriot, this man holds the distinction of being a signer of both the *Declaration of Independence* and the *Constitution*. Read has the unique distinction of being the only man to sign the *Declaration of Independence* who, during the final congressional vote on July 2, 1776, had voted, against independence. A devout Christian all of his life, Read studied at the seminary in New London under Reverend Allison. His father-in-law was pastor for 50 years of the Immanuel Episcopal Church in Newcastle.

5

Turkey, Goose and Chicken – Past Christmas Favorites

Roast Turkey –

Mary Edwards Walker Made it this Way

Carefully wash turkey both inside and out with cold water. Dry turkey and then rub all over with salt and pepper. Pack lightly with favorite stuffing [the Walker family sometimes enjoyed an Oyster Stuffing similar to that made by the Hill family as can be found in Chapter 6] and sew up opening. Put turkey breast facing up on rack in roasting pan. Cover breast with thick bacon slices and sear at 500 degrees for about 15 minutes. Lower heat to 300 degrees and remove bacon strips. Roast turkey until tender. Remember to baste turkey with pan drippings about every 10 to 15 minutes. Allow 25 minutes roasting time for each pound of turkey weight.

Mary Edwards Walker's Own Turkey Stuffing

"Chop together the liver of the turkey and 1 small onion; stir these in a saucepan over the fire, but do not brown, for about 10 minutes; then mix the contents into a pound of sausage meat; when thoroughly mixed, add about 2 dozen whole chestnuts which have been shelled, blanched and cooked until tender in boiling, salted water."

** ** ** ** **

Mary Edwards Walker (1832-1919) was the *only* woman and *only* civilian to be awarded the **Medal of Honor** during the Civil War. This devout Christian woman was a Union Army surgeon who had worked as a nurse on the battlefield because the powers to be would not hire female doctors. Her **Medal of Honor** cites her marvelous efforts at First Manassas. She started at the Battle of Chickamauga on September 19, 1863. There she served in an army hospital in Chattanooga, Tennessee, where she tirelessly toiled as a volunteer surgeon. Dr. Walker often crossed into enemy territory to assist victims in need of her medical skills. She was once taken prisoner on April 10, 1864, when she accidentally walked into a group of Confederate soldiers. Doctor Walker was released soon after in a trade for a Confederate officer and was thereby able to help as a surgeon during the Siege of Atlanta. After the Civil War finally ended, General W. T. Sherman recommended Dr. Walker for the **Medal of Honor**. She was given the award in January of 1866. This great lady proudly wore her medal every day until she died.

Roast Goose –

A Pulaski Christmas Favorite in America

1 Goose

1 cup celery, diced	3 tbls butter, melted
2 garlic cloves, minced	½ tsp cinnamon
½ cup onion, minced	1 tbls honey, warmed
2 cups bread crumbs, dry	2 cups hot water

Put celery, minced garlic, onion and dry bread crumbs in a wooden mixing bowl and blend well. Stir in the melted butter, cinnamon, warmed honey and hot water. Work with fingers until everything is thoroughly blended. Add more hot water if necessary until desired consistency of stuffing is obtained. Now fill cavity of goose with stuffing. Sew cavity together with heavy thread. Place goose, breast side up, on rack in open roasting pan. Bake at 350 degrees for about 3-1/2 hours. Baste frequently with a mixture made with:

2 cups boiling water   1 cup honey

¼ cup vinegar

Add cornstarch to liquid left in bottom of roasting pan. Stir to thicken nicely for a delicious gravy.

** ** ** ** **

Count Casimir Pulaski (1748-79) is seldom, if ever, mentioned in American history textbooks. He was a man who should certainly never be forgotten! This great Christian military leader came to the Colonies from Poland in July of 1777. Pulaski was an idealist who was prepared to fight and die for the cause of liberty and freedom in America. This Polish patriot, asking for nothing in return, donated more than $50, 000 of his own money to form the famed "Pulaski Legion." Imagine how much this would be in dollars today! General Pulaski also offered his services and those of his fighting men to General George Washington at no charge. And in the end, he heroically gave his life for the American cause at the age of only 31 during the Siege of Savannah.

Roasted Chicken Pieces –
The Lewis Family's Christmas Receipt

3 pound frying chicken	2 cups bread crumbs
¾ cup salt pork, minced	Salt to suit taste
3 eggs, well beaten	Pepper to suit taste
3 tbls water	2 tbls butter

Flour as required

Cut frying chicken into suitable pieces for frying and set aside momentarily. Put minced salt pork in a heavy roasting pan and cook until crispy and nicely browned. Blend beaten eggs with the water in a small wooden mixing bowl. Season to suit taste with salt and pepper. Now dip chicken pieces in the egg mixture. Roll each piece in bread crumbs. Put chicken pieces in roasting pan. Let them brown slowly. Season with salt and pepper. Dot each piece with butter. Cover roasting pan. Bake at 325 degrees for about 3 hours or until chicken is tender. Remove chicken. Stir in flour, a tablespoon at a time, to drippings left in roasting pan until a medium thick gravy is achieved. Serve with the chicken. Makes 6 nice servings.

** ** ** ** **

Francis Lewis (1713-1802), the only child of a minister, was born in Wales and orphaned at an early age. Raised by relatives, he eventually ended up in America and became deeply involved in the

Revolutionary movement. He was a member of the Continental Congress from 1775 to 1779. Instructed to not sign the *Declaration of Independence* because of Tory dominance in New York, Lewis ignored them and went ahead and signed anyway on August 2, 1776. Yes, he was yet another of the heroic men in early America who paid dearly for his beliefs in liberty and freedom. In retaliation for his "traitorous" deed against the Crown, the vengeful British invaded Long Island and made a surprise raid on his home in Whitestone while he was away. They ransacked the place and destroyed everything. Not satisfied with this, they brutally beat his wife, took her into custody, and threw her in prison. She died a short time after being released in a 1778 prisoner exchange for wives of British officials. The terrible hardships the British had forced this woman to endure had ruined her health and brought about her early death in 1779. Yet through all of the horrible trials and tribulations, this great Christian patriot never once was known to falter. His faith carried him through it all. Sadly enough, when this great American died, at the age of 89, in New York city, he was buried in an *unmarked grave* in the Trinity Church yard.

Goose and Dumplings –
John Paul Jones Ate this for Christmas

Select a nice plump goose. Dress and then cut into pieces suitable for serving. Place in large kettle and cover with water. Add 1 tablespoon salt and ¼ teaspoon pepper. Cover kettle and let slowly simmer until goose is tender. Meanwhile, prepare dumpling dough as follows:

2 cups flour   4 tsp baking powder

1 tbls salt   2 tbls shortening

     Milk as required

Sift together in a wooden mixing bowl the flour, salt and baking powder. Cut in shortening with 2 spatulas or a fork. Add enough milk until thick drop batter is obtained. Drop batter by teaspoonfuls into boiling broth in kettle. Cover kettle closely. Let boil 12 minutes. Serve goose and dumplings immediately.

** ** ** ** **

John Paul Jones (1747-92) was born in Scotland under the name of John Paul. He was involved in the slave trade between 1766 and 1777 and then relocated to Virginia where he took on the name of John Paul Jones. Congress commissioned him as a naval officer in 1775 and he was almost immediately given command of his own ship. He became a notable during the Revolutionary War because of his daring exploits. This great Christian patriot is widely acclaimed to be the *"Father of the American Navy"* because of his inspirational and heroic deeds at sea. After the War for American Independence was won, Jones, always the adventurer, went on to serve as an Admiral in the Russian navy. A true American hero, John Paul Jones died in obscurity.

Chicken Oyster Gumbo –
A Butterfield Christmas Special

3 pound chicken	1 tomato, sliced
Salt as needed	2 quarts hot water
Pepper as needed	Pinch cayenne pepper
3 tbls lard	24 oysters
3 tbls flour	3 sprigs parsley, minced
3/4 onion, minced	2 tbls file

Cut chicken into pieces suitable for serving. Wash and wipe dry. Season highly with salt and pepper. Melt lard in large kettle. When hot, drop in chicken pieces and fry until browned on all sides. Remove chicken. Sift flour into the melted lard in kettle. Stir and let it brown nicely. Add onion and let it brown slightly. Now stir in tomato slices. Cook 2 minutes, stirring all the while. Add chicken pieces and 2 quarts hot water. Toss in a few grains of cayenne pepper. Let everything simmer until chicken is tender. Then add oysters and parsley. Let simmer 20 more minutes. Take kettle from fire. Lastly, stir in the file. Scoop over boiled or steamed rice and serve while piping hot. *Note: File is made from the tender leaves of the sassafras tree that has been dried and pulverized.*

** ** ** ** **

Daniel Butterfield (1831-1901), A New York merchant, became a Union Brigadier General in September of 1861. He was awarded the **Medal of Honor** for his heroic actions under fire at Gaine's Mill. This notable Christian leader was also Chief-of Staff to General Joseph Hooker and General George Meade in 1863-1864. And he led a division in General Sherman's historic 1864 March to the Sea. But this man, at age 31, did the one thing he would be most remembered for in history. He composed the notes for the famous bugle call we know even today as *"Taps."* He wrote this at Harrison's Landing, Virginia, to be played at funerals and at lights out.

Chicken Fricassee –

A Dish Stonewall Jackson Loved

3-Pound chicken	2 tsp salt
1 large onion, sliced	½ tsp pepper
2 cloves	2 cups flour
¼ bay leaf	½ cup salt pork fat

Cut up the chicken in suitable serving sizes. Carefully wash and rinse with cold water. Put in kettle with 1 quart water. Add sliced onion, cloves and piece of bay leaf. Simmer slowly until chicken is tender. Meanwhile, blend salt, pepper and flour in a wooden mixing bowl. Heat salt pork fat in a large cast iron skillet. Take chicken pieces from kettle. Dredge generously in flour mixture. Put dredged pieces in skillet. Fry until nicely browned on all sides. When done, take chicken pieces and drain on paper. Then neatly arrange pieces on large warmed platter. Add flour mixture to stock in kettle in which chicken was cooked. Stir to thicken. Add salt and pepper to suit taste. Pour this gravy over chicken on platter and serve while hot.

** ** ** ** **

Confederate General Thomas Jonathan "Stonewall" Jackson (1824-63), a brilliant battlefield commander, died when only 39 years old on May 2. He was on reconnaissance at dusk when one of his own men accidentally shot him. Jackson died eight days later, his death a great tragedy for the Confederacy. Approximately 8 months earlier, in September of 1862, Harpers Ferry surrendered to General Jackson. He stopped his horse in front of the 9th Vermont, took off his hat and quietly said: *"Boys, don't feel bad. You couldn't help it. It was just as God willed it."* Stonewall Jackson was General Robert E. Lee's most trusted corps commander in the Army of Northern Virginia. This devout Christian leader wrote to his wife in 1859: *"Is there not comfort in prayer, which is not elsewhere to be found?"*

Chicken Croquettes –

A Tyler Christmas Breakfast Treat

2 cups cooked chicken, chopped	1/8 tsp pepper
	¼ tsp celery salt
1 egg yolk, beaten	Pinch of paprika
¾ cup thick white sauce	2 tbls water
1 tsp lemon juice	1 egg white
½ tsp salt	1 cup cracker crumbs

Take a large wooden mixing bowl and put in chopped chicken, beaten egg yolk, white sauce, lemon juice, salt, pepper, celery salt and paprika. Blend all ingredients thoroughly. Form into small cones, cylinders or flat cakes. Set aside momentarily. Now stir together in a separate bowl the water and egg white. Dip each chicken croquette in egg white mixture. Then roll it in cracker crumbs, then the egg white mixture once again. Fry in deep fat for about 2 minutes. Drain on crumpled absorbent paper. Put on plates and garnish with buttered peas or asparagus tips.

** ** ** ** **

John Tyler (1790-1862) was the 10th President of the United States who served his country in this position from 1841 to 1845. Tyler, a devout Christian, was married for nearly 30 years to Letitia Christian who died in the White House in 1842. They had 8 children. He later at the age of 54, married 23 year old Julia Gardiner in a private church ceremony. Tyler's enemies mocked his May-December marriage, but it was a long and happy one. They had seven more children. After his term in office, Tyler lived in retirement until the Civil War broke out. He then became a delegate to the Provisional Congress of the Confederacy and was denounced in the North as a traitor.

6

Yesteryear's Stuffings for Christmas Birds

Giblet Walnut Stuffing –
As Enjoyed with Turkey by the Monroes

1 cup chopped giblets	2 eggs, well beaten
2 cups bread crumbs	½ cup walnuts, chopped
2 tbls onions, diced	Turkey broth as required
3 tbls celery, cut up	Salt to suit taste
½ tsp parsley, chopped	Pepper to suit taste

Combine in a wooden mixing bowl the giblets, bread crumbs, diced onions, celery and parsley. Stir together. Add the beaten eggs and work in with the fingers until nicely blended. Now add the walnuts. Work them in thoroughly. Then add turkey leavings (broth from roasting pan), a little at a time, until desired consistency of dressing is reached. Add salt and pepper as needed to suit individual taste.

** ** ** ** **

James Monroe (1758-1831), a Christian since childhood, was home schooled by the Reverend William Douglas. He served as a lieutenant colonel in the Continental Army during the early years of the Revolutionary War and was wounded at Trenton, New Jersey. Monroe was sometime later credited with writing our magnificent *Constitution*. He eventually got into national politics under the sponsorship of his friend, Thomas Jefferson, and ultimately became the 5th President of the United States. Monroe was also a member of the Constitutional Convention, served as Secretary of State, Secretary of War, and Minister to France, Great Britain and Spain. He helped negotiate the *Louisiana Purchase* from Napoleon, doubling the size of the United States at that time. And he brought about the *Monroe Doctrine,* a law banning European nations from coming over and creating problems with nations in our hemisphere. Yes, James Monroe was a Christian as were so many of our other Founding Fathers. In his inaugural address on March 4, 1817, he referred to God's overruling providence: ***"Except the Lord keep the city, the watchman waketh in vain."***

Pork Sausage Stuffing –

As Made by Mrs. Gerry for Christmas

1-1/2 pounds pork sausage   1 tbls lemon juice

1-1/2 cups bread crumbs   Salt to suit taste

1 tsp sage, powdered   Pepper to suit taste

Hot water sufficient to moisten

Put sausage, bread crumbs, sage and lemon juice in a wooden mixing bowl. Blend all ingredients thoroughly. Add salt and pepper to suit taste. Slowly add hot water to mixture. Work this in until suitably moistened. **Note:** *This is an excellent stuffing for any kind of roast fowl. According to Mrs. Gerry, bread crumbs are best for use in any stuffing when stale bread is first thoroughly dried out in the oven. Then it is to be crushed by rolling over with a rolling pin before using.*

** ** ** ** **

Elbridge Gerry (1744-1814) of Massachusetts is often a forgotten man in American history, but he shouldn't be when his accomplishments are noted. Gerry, one of the heroic 56 signers of the *Declaration of Independence,* was a prosperous merchant who worked closely with John Hancock, Samuel Adams and John Adams in the American cause for independence. This devout Christian Founding Father also signed the *Articles of Confederation.* He was a delegate to the Constitutional Convention in Philadelphia where he was known to have spoken 119 times. Of the 42 delegates present at the end of the Constitutional Convention on September 17, 1787, all but three signed the *Constitution.* The three who refused were George Mason, John Randolph and Gerry. These three men were all fearful of a powerful centralized government. Gerry went on to become the Vice-President of the United States under President James Madison from 1813 to 1814.

Chestnut Stuffing –

The Pearson Family's Best for Christmas

4 cups chestnuts, blanched	Pepper to suit taste
1/2 cup cream	1 cup butter, melted
Salt to suit taste	2 cups dry bread crumbs

Mash chestnuts in large wooden mixing bowl. Add cream and stir until well mixed. Salt and pepper to suit taste. In a separate bowl, pour melted butter over bread crumbs. Stir until nicely blended. Add this to chestnut-cream mixture in first bowl and blend together thoroughly. This stuffing is excellent for turkey, duck, goose or chicken.

** ** ** ** **

Theodore Pearson was an honest, hard-working Christian businessman in the bustling Colonies of long ago. Pearson won't be remembered for signing the *Declaration of Independence* or the *Constitution*. Nor for attending or speaking at a Constitutional Convention. He probably didn't even know any of the great men who did! Yet, if not for Theodore Pearson, we may not have crackers in our supermarkets today. This man has the distinction of opening America's first cracker factory in Newburyport, Massachusetts, way back in 1792. He was a fellow who attended church regularly, taught Sunday school, and always made a special effort to help those in need. Mr. Pearson, a generous man, personally took it upon himself to see that no family went without food over the Christmas holiday period. Yes, understandably forgotten with the passage of time, Theodore Pearson was an important man nonetheless.

Oyster Stuffing –

As Made for the Rutledge Family

12 large oysters	1 tsp salt
1-1/2 cups oyster liquor	½ tsp pepper
1 egg	1 tbls parsley, chopped
1 egg yolk	2 tbls butter, melted

Dry bread crumbs as required

Cut oysters in quarters and put in wooden mixing bowl with the oyster liquor (juice). Stir in the egg, egg yolk, salt, pepper, parsley and melted butter. Blend all ingredients well. Lastly, work in enough dry bread crumbs to make consistency desired for stuffing the turkey or other fowl.

** ** ** ** **

Edward Rutledge (1749-1800), was a young fellow from a prominent South Carolina family with a good Christian upbringing. He was only 26 years of age when he signed the *Declaration of Independence*. Rutledge

78

was its youngest signer, while Benjamin Franklin on the other hand, at 70, was the oldest. John Adams scathingly characterized the delegates with his busy pen. Regarding Rutledge, he noted not so flatteringly, that Edward was an *"uncouth and ungraceful speaker ... and speaks through his nose ...* "Nevertheless, all of the signers were patriotic, public-spirited citizens who were materially well off -- respected doctors, educators, wealthy farmers, prosperous merchants, etc. Imagine the courage it must have taken for such a young man to sign what was in effect his death warrant should the British have won the war.

Corn Meal Stuffing –

A Paine Family Christmas Favorite

2 cups turkey broth	½ cup onion, diced
½ cup corn meal	1 egg, beaten
3 cups bread crumbs	Sage to suit taste
1 cup celery, diced	Salt to suit taste
1 cup walnut pieces	Pepper to suit taste

Put turkey broth in kettle and bring to boil. Then slowly stir in corn meal so as not to let it get lumpy. Cook 10 minutes. Add bread crumbs, diced celery, walnut pieces, onion and beaten egg. Blend all ingredients well. Season to taste with sage, salt and pepper. Add a little more turkey broth or warm water if needed to get desired consistency of stuffing.

** ** ** ** **

Thomas Paine (1737-1809) fanned the flames of Colonial independence with his December 23, 1776, essay **"The American Crisis."** General George

Washington ordered that this be read aloud to the Colonial Army troops at Valley Forge. In it, Paine wrote: *"Tyranny, like hell, is not easily conquered; yet we have this consolation with us, that the harder the conflict, the more glorious the triumph. ... The cause of America is the cause of all mankind. Where say some, is the King of America? I'll tell you, friend, He reigns above. ..."* Thomas Paine called himself an *"Englishman by birth, French citizen by decree, and American by adoption."* His last words before dying were: *"I die in perfect composure and resignation to the will of my Creator, God."*

Oyster Pecan Stuffing –
The Hill Family's Christmas Receipt

1 cup oysters, quartered	½ cup pecan pieces
2 cups soft bread crumbs	½ tsp parsley flakes
¼ cup onions, diced	3 tbls butter, melted
½ cup celery, diced	Salt to suit taste
¼ cup green pepper, diced	Pepper to suit taste
1 egg, well beaten	Oyster liquor as needed
Turkey broth as needed	

Put oysters in a large wooden mixing bowl. Add soft bread crumbs, diced onions, celery, green pepper and well beaten egg. Blend everything well. Then add pecan pieces and parsley flakes. Stir in the melted butter and again blend everything thoroughly. Add salt and pepper to suit taste. Lastly, add some of the liquor (juice) left from the oysters, a little at a time. Work it in by kneading mixture with fingers. Continue until desired consistency of stuffing is reached. If more liquid is required, use turkey broth from the roasting pan, or a little warm water.

** ** ** ** **

Daniel Harvey Hill (1821-89), raised by a fundamental Baptist family in South Carolina, spent seven years fighting in the Mexican War after graduating from West Point. He resigned his commission in the

United States Army when the Civil War started and joined with the Confederacy. As a Major General in March of 1862, Hill commanded a division fighting at Seven Pines, the Seven Days Battles and at South Mountain. He was in charge of defending Richmond during the Gettysburg Campaign and was a prominent military leader at both Chickamauga and Chattanooga. Hill's downfall apparently came when he signed a petition recommending that General Braxton Bragg be removed from his command due to incompetence. But politics being as they always are, a great military leader, proven under fire, was virtually destroyed. Instead of Bragg being removed as should have been the case, Hill instead was relieved of his command and transferred to an obscure post in North Carolina. There he eventually surrendered to Union forces with General J. E. Johnston.

Mushroom Stuffing –

The Greene Family's Best

1 cup mushrooms, chopped	½ cup celery, diced
2 cups bread crumbs, soft	½ tsp parsley, chopped
½ cup walnut pieces	3 tbls turkey fat, minced
¼ cup onion, diced	Salt to suit taste
	Pepper to suit taste
	2 eggs, well beaten
Turkey broth as required	

Put chopped mushrooms, bread crumbs, walnut pieces, diced onion, celery and chopped parsley in a large wooden mixing bowl. Blend all ingredients thoroughly. Then stir in minced turkey fat. Add salt and pepper to suit taste. Add beaten eggs and work in with fingers. Lastly, add turkey broth, a little at a time, working it in by kneading mixture with fingers. Continue this until desired consistency of stuffing is reached.

** ** ** ** **

Nathaniel Greene (1742-86) was an outstanding officer in General Washington's Continental Army in 1775. He was a Quaker from Rhode Island, but was disowned quickly by his religious sect because of his military leanings. Greene organized three regiments of militia in Rhode Island as *"an Army of Observation"* right after the Lexington affair. On June 22, 1775, he was commissioned a Brigadier General in the Continental Army. Washington saw and appreciated Greene's military expertise and leadership qualities. He soon after promoted him to Major General in August of 1776. Never faltering in his strong Christian convictions, Greene fought at Trenton as well as in Virginia, North Carolina and South Carolina. He returned to Rhode Island when the war ended.

7

Cider Baked Ham and Other Meat Specials for Christmas

Salt Cured Cider Baked Ham –

As Prepared for the Pinckney Family

1 small lean country ham

Wash ham thoroughly in lukewarm water. Then soak overnight in cold water. Wipe dry the next morning. Sprinkle over the flesh side of the ham a mixture of:

1 tbls onion, chopped fine	1 tbls cinnamon
¼ tsp mace	1 tbls allspice
¼ tsp cloves	

Now make a simple paste dough with flour and water. Roll out in thin sheet. Cover flesh side of ham. Pack dough down close to skin. Put ham, skin side down, in large roasting pan. Now you will need the following ingredients:

2 quarts cider	1 egg, well beaten
½ tsp white pepper	Bread crumbs as needed
½ tsp paprika	Chopped parsley, as needed

Pour cider into roasting pan with ham. Stir in white pepper and paprika. Cover with another large pan. Bake at 350 degrees for 2 hours. Baste every 20 minutes. At the end of 2 hours, remove upper pan and allow ham to cook 2 more hours uncovered. When done, take from oven and remove paste dough. Take off all the skin. Neatly trim ham. Brush skin side with beaten egg. Dust with fine bread crumbs and chopped parsley. Then put back in oven at 450 degrees to brown nicely.

** ** ** ** **

Thomas Pinckney (1750-1828) fought with the Continental Army under General Washington during the War for American Independence. This great Christian leader from a prominent South Carolina family was wounded during the Battle of Camden and taken prisoner by the British. Pinckney served as Governor of South Carolina after the war was over. He was the man who presided over the convention that ratified the *Constitution*. Educated in England as a young man, he was later appointed as Minister to Great Britain and served honorably in that position from 1792 to 1796.

Steak and Bacon Balls –

A Lee Favorite at Christmas

4 bacon slices, cubed	½ tsp pepper
1 cup fine cracker crumbs	¼ cup onion, minced
½ cup hot water	¼ cup celery, minced
1 cup steak, ground	¼ tsp thyme
1 egg, slightly beaten	¼ tsp sage
1/2 tsp salt	¼ tsp allspice

Flour as required

Put cubed bacon slices in cast iron skillet and sauté until crisp. Add cracker crumbs and stir until nicely browned. Then add hot water and blend everything nicely. Dump mixture into wooden mixing bowl. Add ground steak, beaten egg, salt, pepper, minced onion and celery, thyme, sage and allspice. Blend all ingredients thoroughly. Form into small balls. Roll in flour. Put balls in well greased cast iron skillet and sauté on all sides. Serve with a gravy made by adding a little flour to the juices left in the skillet. *Note: This same mixture was sometimes used by the Lee family to make a nice meat loaf. If this is done, simply bake at 400 degrees until done.*

** ** ** ** **

General Robert E. Lee (1807-70), a devout Christian leader, will always be looked upon as a hero to the Southern cause. He was the fourth child of Revolutionary War notable, Henry "Lighthorse" Harry Lee. A brilliant young man, he graduated second in his class at West Point. Lee married Mary Custis, the granddaughter of George Washington and Mary Custis Washington. Robert E. Lee once commented: *"In all my perplexities and distresses, the Bible has never failed to give me light and strength."* Stonewall Jackson's Chaplain, B.T. Lacey and Chaplain J. William Jones once paid General Lee a visit in his tent to let him know that all the chaplains were praying for him. Tears came to Lee's eyes as he told them: *"Please thank them for that, sir – I warmly appreciate it. And I can only say that I am nothing but a poor sinner, trusting in Christ alone for salvation, and need all of the prayers they can offer me."*

Bacon Liver Loaf –

As Prepared by Betsy Ross for Christmas

2 pound liver	2 onions, chopped
4 slices bacon	2 tbls parsley, chopped
2 tsp salt	2 eggs, beaten
¼ tsp pepper	2 cups bread crumbs

Put liver and bacon in small kettle. Cover with water. Bring to boil and let simmer for from 8 to 10 minutes. Drain and save water. Then take from kettle and grind liver and bacon together. Put mixture in wooden mixing bowl. Add salt, pepper, chopped onions and parsley. Then work in eggs. Set aside momentarily. Put bread crumbs on baking sheet and dry in oven. When nicely browned, add these to mixture in bowl. Blend everything thoroughly. Press into well greased loaf pan. Bake at 350 to 375 degrees for about 40 minutes or until browned. Turn loaf out on hot platter. Pour heated water in which liver and bacon was boiled over the loaf. Serve immediately. Makes enough to serve 6 people.

** ** ** ** **

Betsy Ross (1752-1836) was one of 17 children who were raised in a staunch Quaker family. Her father, Samuel Grissom, a carpenter, helped to build Independence Hall in Philadelphia where the *Declaration of Independence* was signed by John Hancock, Thomas Jefferson and all of the other great American patriots. . She married John Ross, a non-Quaker, and was expelled from her sect. Betsy was a twice-widowed seamstress of 25 who lived in Philadelphia when she was asked to make our first flag. According to her grandson, this very attractive woman produced the first Stars and Stripes in 1776 when: *"A band of Continental leaders called upon my grandmother and asked her to undertake a special task. They probably selected her because George Washington was one of her patrons; she sewed many shirt ruffles for him about the time he was made Commander-in-Chief."*

Stuffed Flank Steaks –

Beauregard's Christmas Favorite

12 medium potatoes	3 tbls bacon drippings
2 tbls butter	1 tsp salt
½ cup cream	½ tsp pepper
1 onion, minced	1 tsp poultry seasoning
2 1-1/2 to 2 pound flank steaks	

Wash potatoes and put in large kettle, skins and all. Cover with water. Bring to a boil. Cook until potatoes are soft. When done, mash thoroughly. Blend in the butter and cream. Set aside momentarily. Now put minced onion in a cast iron skillet with bacon drippings. Sauté until soft and lightly browned. Add this to potato mixture in the skillet. Stir in salt, pepper and poultry seasoning. Again set aside while preparing flank steaks. Put one steak on top of the other. Sew edges together with coarse white twine, leaving one edge open. Stuff with the potato dressing in kettle. Then close steak by sewing the open end together. Lay in roasting pan. Sprinkle top of steak with salt and pepper. Dot with butter. Bake at 350 degrees until tender. Baste often with melted butter. Add a little water to roasting pan to make gravy. Thicken when steak is done by stirring a little flour in with liquid in bottom of pan. Serve on warm platter. Surround steak with hot buttered peas.

** ** ** ** **

Pierre Gustave Toutant Beauregard (1818-93) was a brilliant Confederate General during the Civil War. Born into a wealthy Louisiana Creole family, he graduated second in his class at West Point in 1838. Beauregard, a professed Christian, became the new Confederacy's first hero with his successful military assault on Fort Sumter. He always went by the name of P.G.T. Beauregard which is quite understandable with all of those unique and sometimes difficult to pronounce names. Beauregard saw much action at such places as Charleston, the Battle of First Manassas, Bull Run, Shiloh and Petersburg. Highly thought of as a military tactician and leader, he rejected numerous offers of senior command positions in the Egyptian Army after the War Between the States ended. He instead returned to Louisiana and ran the New Orleans, Jackson & Mississippi Railway for a period of five years. Beauregard was also in charge of the Louisiana Lottery and in 1888 became the Commissioner of Public Works in New Orleans.

Christmas Meat Loaf –
As Made by Mrs. John Hunt Morgan

3 pounds round steak	2 eggs, well beaten
½ pound veal	2 cups bread
½ pound salt pork	crumbs
2 large onions,	2 tbls parsley,
chopped fine	minced
2 green peppers,	2-1/2 tsp salt
chopped fine	½ tsp pepper
½ tsp paprika	

Put steak, veal and salt pork through meat grinder together. Grind into large wooden mixing bowl. Then thoroughly blend in the chopped onions, green peppers, beaten eggs and bread crumbs. Season with parsley, salt, pepper and paprika. Shape into a nice loaf. Place in well-greased baking pan. Bake at 400 degrees for 45 minutes. When done, place on hot platter and serve with gravy made from juices left in baking pan. Gravy can be made by simply adding a little flour to juices and stirring until it begins to thicken. *Note: This meat loaf is equally delicious when eaten cold as a snack.*

** ** ** ** **

John Hunt Morgan (1825-64) enlisted in the Confederate Army and became a scout when the Civil War broke out. So talented was he that he soon after commanded the Kentucky cavalry as a colonel at Shiloh in April of 1862. This young *Bible* believing Christian became known as a raider, taking 400 prisoners in Mississippi and Tennessee. Rewarded by being given command of a brigade, he started out on July 4th with 800 men on a bold raid into Union territory. Covering 1000 miles in 24 days, he and his men captured 1200 Union prisoners while losing less than 100 of his own raiders. Then in December of 1862, during the Stones River Campaign, Morgan's Raiders captured 1800 prisoners and destroyed more than 2 million dollars worth of Union military supplies. Only two of his men were killed and 24 were wounded. This heroic exploit earned him a promotion to Brigadier General and the command of a cavalry division. Morgan was finally captured by Federal troops in Lisbon, Ohio, on July 26. He escaped from the Ohio penitentiary in November and again initiated his famous raids. But John Hunt Morgan's luck ran out and he was killed in Greenville, Tennessee, on September 4, 1864.

Stuffed Heart –

As Enjoyed by the Adams' Family

2 Calf hearts	1 green pepper, chopped
or	3 cups bread crumbs
1 Beef heart	1 cup celery, chopped
4 tbls bacon drippings	½ tsp salt
1 onion, chopped	1/8 tsp pepper

Wash the calf hearts or the beef heart in cold water and carefully remove the gristle and veins. Make a slit in the side and fill with stuffing made as follows: Heat bacon drippings in a cast iron skillet. Then stir in the chopped onion and green pepper. Sauté for a few minutes until both are soft. Add bread crumbs, chopped celery, salt and pepper. Blend everything thoroughly. Sprinkle heart inside and out liberally with salt and pepper. Fill with hot stuffing from skillet. Now put heart in skillet and sear on both sides. Place in baking pan. Add ½ cup water. Cover and bake at 300 degrees until tender. A beef heart will take about 2 hours. A calf heart will be tender in a much shorter time. Remove heart when done. Add a little flour to drippings and enough water to make thin gravy. Serve baked heart surrounded by gravy. *Note: John Adams always preferred the calf hearts to a beef heart when they were available.*

** ** ** ** **

John Adams (1735-1826) was a patriot and leader in the Colonies with his cousin, Samuel Adams, for more than 20 years prior to the American Revolution. He was a member of the Continental Congress and a signer of the *Declaration of Independence*. As Minister to France, he along with Benjamin Franklin and John Jay assisted in the negotiations for a treaty with England to end the Revolutionary War. He was a major force behind getting the American states to ratify the *Constitution*. Commenting on the signing of the *Declaration of Independence*, Adams said in part: ***"It ought to be commemorated, as a Day of Deliverance, by solemn acts of devotion to God Almighty."***

Leg of Lamb –

A Caesar Rodney Christmas Treat

6 pound leg of lamb, bone still in	1 tsp thyme
	Pepper as needed
2 large garlic cloves, slivered	4 cups new potatoes
	4 cups fresh carrots
1 tsp salt	2 cups small onions
1 tsp rosemary	3 tbls lemon juice

Carefully make a number of slits in the leg of lamb and insert slivers of garlic. Blend salt, rosemary and thyme in a cup. Rub this mixture over leg of lamb. Then liberally sprinkle with pepper. Put half the potatoes, carrots and onions in bottom of large cooking pot. Now lay in leg of lamb. Place remaining vegetables over this. Sprinkle lemon juice on the mixture. Cover and cook slowly in oven at 200 degrees. For rare: about 6 hours. For well done: about 8 to 10 hours. When finished cooking, take leg of lamb from pot and place on warm platter. Serve with vegetables heaped all around.

** ** ** ** **

Caesar Rodney (1728-84), a Delaware signer of the *Declaration of Independence*, was the 47 year old son of a wealthy 800-acre plantation owner near Dover in Kent County. This dedicated Christian patriot had to cover his head with a green silk scarf to hide the horrible cancer that was eating away his face. A fellow signer described him as: *"An animated skeleton with a bandaged head."*

Yet, despite his physically weakened condition, Rodney was not to be denied his place in history. He bravely rode 80 miles by horseback, all night through a terrible thunderstorm, in order to be in Philadelphia in time to join his colleagues in signing the historic *Declaration*. Rodney later spent much of his time recruiting troops to fight in the War for Independence. He was commissioned a major general in September of 1777 and fought the British in Delaware and New Jersey.

8

Christmas Desserts of Olden Times

Boiled Custard –
As Made for Lincoln as a Boy

1 quart milk	Pinch of salt
4 egg whites	¾ cup sugar
4 egg yolks	Vanilla to suit taste

Pour milk into saucepan and heat. Beat egg whites until they are stiff and lay on top of milk in saucepan. Skim frothy egg whites off onto flat dish just before milk begins to boil. Carefully drain off any milk from egg whites. Now beat egg yolks in wooden mixing bowl until they are light. Stir hot milk into them. Pour mixture back into saucepan. Heat while stirring until it nearly boils and starts to thicken. Stir in salt, sugar and vanilla. Spoon into bowl and lay fluffy egg whites on top. This boiled custard is delicious when eaten either hot or cold.

** ** ** ** **

Abraham Lincoln's (1809-65) last law partner, William H. Herndon, once commented that the future President *"had a good appetite ... ate mechanically, never asking why such a thing was not on the table nor why it was on it ... he filled up and that is all."* Although this may be true, Lincoln must have had a few favorites from childhood. His stepmother, Mrs. Thomas Lincoln used to make him a boiled custard dish that no child could ever forget. It was mostly made to celebrate holidays and was always on the table at Christmas. The recipe given above is exactly as she made it for him. Lincoln was a devout Christian man who had this to say about the *Bible*: *"In regard to this Great Book, I have but to say, I believe the Bible is the best gift God has given to man. All the good Saviour gave to the world was communicated through this Book. But for this Book we could not know right from wrong. All things most desirable for man's welfare, here and hereafter, are to be found portrayed in it."*

Christmas Plum Pudding –
The Rush Family's Best Holiday Dessert

2 cups butter	½ tbls cloves
2 cups sugar	½ tbls mace
12 egg yolks, beaten	2 tbls nutmeg
2 cups milk	12 cups raisins, chopped,
10 cups flour	dredged in flour
12 egg whites, beaten	1 cup citron, shredded,
1 cup brandy	dredged in flour

1 pound suet, chopped fine

Cream butter and sugar and large wooden mixing bowl. Stir in beaten egg yolks, then the milk. Next add flour, alternately, with stiffly beaten egg whites. Then stir in brandy, cloves, mace and nutmeg. Lastly work in the raisins, citron and chopped suet. Thoroughly blend all ingredients. Dip a heavy muslin cloth (called a "pudding cloth" in the old days) in hot water and wring it out. Flour inside of the cloth well. Then put mixture from bowl in this cloth and tie the end. Place in large kettle of hot water and let it boil for 5 hours. When done, lift it out and dip at once in cold water. Let stand to cool slightly. Remove pudding from cloth and serve while hot. Any leftover plum pudding can be sliced and fried in butter for a delicious breakfast treat. *Note: Plum pudding, when placed on the table in the Rush household, was always lit with rum or brandy just before being served. The blue flame represented the fire of hell. When it died down it symbolized good winning over evil. Mrs. Rush, as did many others in her day, used holly to decorate her plum pudding dish after it was cooked. The red berries represented the blood of Jesus.*

** ** ** ** **

Benjamin Rush (1745-1813) was a Pennsylvania signer of the *Declaration of Independence*. He served as Surgeon General in the Continental Army in 1777 but resigned after a tiff with George Washington. When the Revolutionary War ended, this man set up the first free medical clinic in America. Rush became the most famous physician and medical teacher in the country. In describing himself, this devout Christian had this to say: *"I have alternately been called an Aristocrat and a Democrat. I am neither, I am a Christocrat."* Rush wrote to his wife during his final illness: *" ... blessed Jesus, wash away all my impurities, and receive me into Thy everlasting kingdom."*

Steamed Christmas Pudding –
The Magruder Family's Yultide Receipt

3 eggs, beaten	½ tsp salt
1 cup brown sugar	1 tsp cinnamon
½ cup molasses	1 tsp cloves
1-1/2 cups bread crumbs, grated	1 tsp nutmeg
	¾ cup grape juice
1-1/2 cups suet, finely chopped	½ cup orange marmalade
2 cups flour	3 cups raisins
1 tsp baking powder	½ cup citron, sliced

Take a large wooden mixing bowl and blend the following: beaten eggs, brown sugar, molasses, grated bread crumbs and finely chopped suet. Sift together in a separate mixing bowl the flour, baking powder, salt, cinnamon, cloves and nutmeg. Stir these dry ingredients, alternately, with the grape juice, into with the ingredients in the first mixing bowl. Then work in the marmalade. Now dredge the raisins and citron in flour. Add these to the mixture and blend everything thoroughly. Place in well-greased pudding mold. Cover tightly. Steam for 3 hours. Serve with Hard Sauce or other pudding sauce. Makes one very large steamed pudding. *Note: Superstitions abounded when it came to preparing a steamed pudding for the family at Christmas. Many homemakers would only allow the pudding mixture to be stirred clockwise as this was said to bring good luck. Some thought that wishes made while stirring in this manner would eventually be granted. A ring was sometimes added to the ingredients. The person finding the ring in his or her serving was seen as a sign of marriage within a year.*

* ** ** ** **

John Bankhead Magruder (1810-71) was one of the Confederacy's most acclaimed military heroes. He became a celebrity throughout the South because of his significant victory at Big Bethel on June 10, 1861. An 1830 West Point graduate, Magruder resigned his U.S. Army commission in March of 1861 and became a Colonel in the Confederate service. An incredibly good leader, he soon thereafter was promoted to Brigadier and then to Major General in a matter of months. When the Civil War ended, this proud and dedicated Christian officer defiantly refused to ask for a parole. Magruder instead went into exile in Mexico where he became a Major General under Maximilian.

Hard Sauce –

For the Boudinet's Christmas Puddings

1 cup butter   1 cup sugar

1 tsp vanilla

Put butter in small wooden mixing bowl and cream until very light and fluffy. Add sugar gradually while beating. Lastly beat in vanilla.

Mrs. Boudinet's Hot Pudding Sauce

1 cup sugar   2 cups water, boiling

1 tbls flour   1/3 cup butter

1 wine glass of sherry

Put sugar and flour in small wooden mixing bowl and blend well. Gradually add boiling water, continually stirring to prevent mixture from lumping. Let simmer until it thickens nicely. Remove from fire. Beat in butter. Lastly add sherry and blend thoroughly. Serve while hot.

** ** ** ** **

Elias Boudinet (1740-1821) was a highly respected patriot in the American Colonies. He was the Founding Father who in 1783 held the esteemed position as President of the Continental Congress. Nevertheless, most people today remember this great man as being the founder and President of the American *Bible* Society. Boudinet once stated: ***"Good government generally begins in the family, and if the moral character of a people once degenerate, their political character must soon follow."***

Molasses Pudding –

A Longstreet Family Christmas Dish

1 cup flour	1 egg, well beaten
½ tbls sugar	¼ cup butter, melted
½ tsp salt	½ cup molasses
½ tsp baking soda	½ cup buttermilk

Sift together in a wooden mixing bowl the flour, sugar, salt and baking soda. In a separate bowl, put the beaten egg, melted butter and molasses. Blend well. Add dry ingredients from first bowl to this and stir just enough to mix well. Now stir in the buttermilk. Pour mixture into buttered 8-inch square baking pan. Bake at 350 degrees for 20 to 25 minutes or until done. Serve while hot with **Brown Sugar Sauce** as made by Mrs. Longstreet.

Mrs. Longstreet's Brown Sugar Sauce

1 egg white	¼ tsp vanilla
½ cup brown sugar	1 egg yolk, well beaten

Few grains salt   1/3 cup heavy cream

Put egg white in wooden mixing bowl and beat until stiff. Gradually add brown sugar, beating thoroughly after each addition. Add salt, vanilla and well beaten egg yolk. Blend well. Beat the heavy cream in separate bowl until it is thick and fluffy. Lastly, fold this into mixture and spread on molasses pudding. Makes enough to serve 6 people nicely.

** ** ** ** **

Brigadier General James Longstreet (1821-1904) often enjoyed this old "receipt" as a child over the Christmas holidays. He gained a great deal of fame during the Civil War while commanding the Confederate Brigade from Virginia. Longstreet was seriously wounded in May of 1864, just after leading a successful battle against Union forces. He did recover, however, but was unable to return to the battlefront for a number of months. General Longstreet was a devout Christian who once wrote: " ... *I am pleased to say: I believe in God, the Father, and in His only begotten Son, Jesus Christ, our Lord. It is my custom to read one or more chapters of my Bible daily for comfort, guidance, and instruction. Knowing myself a sinner, I am greatly relieved by the happy assurance that for such our Saviour died, and that under lowly penitence He will surely forgive, and make our acceptance certain through His holy pleasure.*"

Mince Meat Pie Filling –
A Ben Franklin Christmas Favorite

4 pounds apples	½ cup molasses
2 pounds lean beef	1-1/2 tsp cinnamon
or veal, chopped	1-1/4 tsp nutmeg
½ pound suet, ground	1 tsp mace
4 pounds raisins	½ tsp cloves
¼ pound citron, ground	2 tsp salt
4 cups brown sugar	Cider as needed

Cut skins from apples, core and chop in tiny pieces. Put into large kettle with chopped beef or veal and ground suet. Heat kettle and stir in raisins, ground citron, brown sugar and molasses. When mixture begins to simmer, stir in cinnamon, nutmeg, mace, cloves and salt. Add cider to moisten nicely. Blend all ingredients thoroughly. Let everything simmer until meat and fruit is tender. Pack while hot in freshly sterilized pint or quart jars. Seal. Store away until ready to use.

** ** ** ** **

As we all know, Benjamin Franklin (1706-1790) worked closely with Thomas Jefferson, John Adams and others on a special committee to develop the *Declaration of Independence.* And Franklin was one of the brave men who stood tall and courageously signed the great *Declaration.* He was also instrumental along with Jefferson and Adams in approving the design of the official seal of the United States. Franklin was the oldest signer at 70, while Edward Rutledge at 26 was the youngest. He was also a signer of the *Constitution.* This great American patriot taught himself five languages and was responsible for bringing France into the Revolutionary War on the side of the Colonies. Franklin once wrote*: "Here is my creed. I believe in one God, the Creator of the Universe. That He governs it by His Providence. That He ought to be worshipped."*

Christmas Fruit Pudding –

A Favorite of "Lighthorse" Harry Lee

2-1/2 cups flour	½ cup butter, melted
¼ tsp baking soda	1 cup molasses
3 tsp baking powder	1-1/2 cups raisins,
½ tsp salt	dredged in flour
½ tsp nutmeg	1 cup milk
½ tsp cinnamon	½ cup cherries, dried

Sift together in a wooden mixing bowl the flour and all other dry ingredients. Then sift a second time. Add the rest of the ingredients in the order given. Blend everything thoroughly. Pour mixture into buttered moulds. Cover tightly and steam for 2 hours. Serve with Hard Sauce or other pudding sauce. Makes 4 small puddings.

** ** ** ** **

Henry "Lighthorse" Harry Lee (1756-1818) was an outstanding General during the Revolutionary War. He was later the Governor of Virginia from 1792 to 1795. Lee was a devout Christian and close personal friend of George Washington. After Washington died at about 10 p.m. on December 14, 1779, this great leader had the honor of delivering the eulogy at the memorial ceremony held in the national capitol, Philadelphia. It was the day after Christmas when Lee gave his never to be forgotten eulogy that contained the words: *"First in war, first in peace and first in the hearts of his countrymen, he was second to none. ... "*

9

Egg Nog, Punch and Other Old-Time Christmas Drinks

Frosted Coffee –

The Pinckney Family's Christmas Drink

2 tbls coffee syrup   1 cup milk

1 heaping tbls vanilla ice cream

Put coffee syrup, milk and ice cream in a shaker or tightly covered canning jar. Shake well. Pour into tall glass. Note: Use only 1 tablespoon coffee syrup if a less sweet drink is preferred.

To Make Coffee Syrup for the Above

2 cups sugar   2 cups strong coffee

Put sugar and coffee in saucepan and stir until sugar is all dissolved. Bring to boil. Let boil 10 minutes without stirring. Set aside to cool. Pour into canning jar and cover. Store in cool place until needed.

** ** ** ** **

Charles Pinckney (1757-1824) was another member of the prominent South Carolina family who played such an important role in formulating and then ratifying the *United States Constitution*. He served in the Continental Army under General George Washington as did his brothers, Charles Cotesworth Pinckney and Thomas Pinckney. Charles, a Christian, as were his brothers, was captured by the British when Charleston fell and was held prisoner until the end of the war. This man later served as a delegate to the Constitutional Convention where he played a most important role. And he also served several terms as Governor of South Carolina.

Egg Nog –

As Enjoyed by Robert Morris

5 egg whites	¼ tsp salt
5 egg yolks	2 tsp vanilla
¼ cup sugar	Nutmeg to suit

Put egg whites in a small wooden mixing bowl and beat them to a soft fluffy peak. Stir in the egg yolks and beat again. Add the sugar, salt and vanilla. Beat a third time. Set aside to chill. When thoroughly chilled, sprinkle with nutmeg and serve.

** ** ** ** **

Robert Morris (1734-1806) of Pennsylvania, widely known as a financial genius, was one of the wealthiest men in the Colonies. He was a Christian patriot, and is best remembered today as *"the financier of the American Revolution."* A merchant by trade, Morris was one of the 56 brave men who signed the *Declaration of Independence.* He and Roger Sherman, another signer of the *Declaration,* were the only two men who also signed the nation's other two basic documents: the *Articles of Confederation* and the *Constitution.* Morris and the others had the courage to take a stand for liberty and freedom. They all clearly understood that they were pledging *"to each other our lives, our fortunes, and our sacred honor."* And they all understood that a noose awaited them if the British were to win the war. Would you be among the courageous signers if asked to do so today? Morris was also a delegate to the Constitutional Convention as well as a member of the Continental Congress. This man, in his later years, ran into serious financial difficulties through numerous bad investments. He was arrested and thrown into Philadelphia's debtors prison in 1798. By the time he was released in 1801, his property and fortune was gone through a Federal bankruptcy law. His health was poor and his spirit broken. This once powerful man finished his life in poverty and relative obscurity until he died.

Fruit Juice Punch –
General Leonidas Polk's Favorite

9 cups water	2 cups orange juice
9 mint leaves	2 cups lemon juice
3 cups sugar	2 cups cherry juice
4 cups tea	2 cups grape juice

Put the water and mint leaves in small cooking pot and bring to quick boil. Let simmer 5 minutes. Take out mint leaves. Stir in the sugar. Again bring to boil. Let simmer 5 more minutes. Set aside to cool. When cooled, add tea and all the fruit juices. Add ice to chill. Makes 4 servings.

** ** ** ** **

Confederate Major General Leonidas Polk's (1806-64) father had fought in the American War for Independence and had been instrumental in founding the University of North Carolina. Polk was a West Point graduate who was a Christian convert while still a cadet. He later resigned his U.S, Army commission to enter the Episcopal ministry. He soon became the Bishop of Louisiana. When the Civil War broke out, Polk was offered a commission as Major General by his friend Jefferson Davis (who had been a cadet with him). He quickly accepted, as he truly believed the South was fighting for a holy cause. Polk went into combat with another close friend, General Albert Sidney Johnston, at

Shiloh in April of 1862. He served the Confederacy while retaining his high position in the church. Polk came to own 400 slaves through an inheritance of his wife and established a Sunday school for them. He was killed during the Atlanta Campaign near Marietta, Georgia, when a sniper shot him from his saddle. All throughout the Civil War his men fondly referred to this kindly man as "Bishop Polk." James Knox Polk, 11th President of the United States was one of his kinsmen.

Christmas Drinks –

Enjoyed by General Wade Hampton

Strawberry Punch

1-1/2 cups strawberry juice	½ cup tea
Juice of 3 lemons	2 cups water

Combine all of the ingredients in a shaker or a canning jar and tightly cap. Shake well. Pour over ice in a tall glass. Serve very cold.

Lemon Frothy

2 eggs	2 cups milk
¾ cup sugar	¼ cup lemon juice

Put eggs and sugar in a wooden mixing bowl. Beat together until light and frothy. Slowly but thoroughly beat in the milk. Lastly, stir in the lemon juice. Pour over ice in a tall glass. Serve very cold.

** ** ** ** **

Confederate General Wade Hampton (1818-1902) was wounded during the first battle of Bull Run. He recovered in time to heroically lead an infantry brigade during the Peninsular Campaign in the Spring of 1862. A fearless warrior, Hampton was known to always have his *Bible* at his side when riding into battle. He was later wounded three more times at Gettysburg. Hampton was one of the wealthiest planters in South Carolina before the Civil War, having been born into an aristocratic Christian family. He fought with J.E.B. Stuart's cavalry corps and rose to become second in command. When Stuart was killed in May of 1864, Hampton was given command of Robert E. Lee's cavalry corps. When the Civil War finally ended, General Hampton returned to his South Carolina estate and made an effort to rebuild his now shrunken fortune. He became involved politically in an effort to thwart the horrendous Radical Republican Reconstruction policies construed by hate-filled Northern politicians to punish the South and its leaders. Hampton was elected Governor in 1876 (defeating a "carpetbagger" incumbent), re-elected in 1878, and then went on to the Senate a short time later.

Hot Buttered Rum –

A Christmas Favorite of Lafayette

Butter to Suit	1 jigger (ounce) rum
1 tsp sugar	1 pat butter
½ mug boiling water	Nutmeg to suit

Rub butter around the inside of a stoneware mug. Put in the sugar and shake it well so it sticks to the bottom and sides. Add boiling water until mug is half full. Stir in the rum and float pat of butter on top. Stir. Sprinkle a little nutmeg on top. Serve while hot. Makes one drink.

** ** ** ** **

Marquis de Lafayette (1757-1834) came over to the Colonies from France to offer his services to General George Washington in the American War for Independence. He volunteered to shed his blood for liberty, and if need be, to give his life for the cause of freedom. Few men in all of history can be found that were braver and less selfish than was this great friend of young America in her desperate time of need. General

Lafayette was a devout Christian who quickly proved his mettle on the battlefield. When he saw the American soldier's plight at Valley Forge he was horrified and wrote: *"They had neither coats, hats, shirts, nor shoes; their feet and legs froze until they became black ... "*

Raspberry Shrub –
The Madison Family's Receipts

4 quarts red raspberries   Vinegar as needed

Sugar as required

Put red raspberries in a stone crock. Add enough vinegar to cover berries. Cover crock loosely and let stand a full 24-hours. Then drain off liquid and discard. Squeeze juice from berries. Measure the amount of juice and put in a kettle. Stir in an equal amount of sugar. Bring mixture to a boil. Let simmer for 20 minutes. Set aside to cool. Bottle when cold and seal with wax. Keep in cool, dark place. When ready to use, dilute with water to taste and serve by pouring over ice.

Or

3 pints red raspberries   1 pint cider vinegar

Sugar as needed

Put red raspberries in stone crock. Add enough cider vinegar to cover berries. Cover loosely and let stand a full 24-hours. Then drain off liquid and discard. Crush berries in crock. Measure amount of juice and put in a kettle. Add 1 pound granulated sugar to every pint of juice in kettle. Bring to boil and then let simmer for 30 minutes. Stir often. Set aside to cool. Bottle when cold and seal with wax. Keep in cool, dark place. When ready to use, dilute with water to taste and serve by pouring over ice.

** ** ** ** **

James Madison (1751-1836) was Secretary of State under Thomas Jefferson as well as the 4th President of the United States from 1809 to 1817. He was a leading member of the Continental Congress. Madison's most important contribution as one of our great Founding Fathers was his work on the writing of the *Constitution.* He is for this reason most often credited by historians as being the *"Father of the Constitution."* Madison, more than any other patriot of his time, pushed the *Bill of Rights* through Congress. This man was unquestionably a Christian. He once said: ***"We have staked the whole future of American civilization ... upon the capacity of mankind ... to sustain ourselves according to the Ten Commandments of God."***

Sherry Egg-Nog –

Von Steuben's Christmas Concoction

1 egg yolk	1 tbls sherry wine
1 tsp sugar	¾ cup cold milk
Pinch of salt	1 egg white, lightly beaten

Nutmeg to suit

Put the egg yolk in small wooden mixing bowl and beat until thick and lemon colored. Stir in the sugar, salt and sherry wine. Add the cold milk. Pour into a shaker or tightly covered canning jar. Shake well. Fold in the fluffy egg whites. Pour into glasses. Sprinkle with nutmeg. Serve cold.

** ** ** ** **

Frederick William Augustus Henry Ferdinand von Steuben (1730-94) was a fine, highly regarded Prussian military strategist. This great Christian patriot came over to the Colonies from Europe and volunteered his services to the emerging nation during the Revolutionary War. He is best remembered for instilling discipline in the

Continental Army at Valley Forge. Inspector General von Steuben believed from the very beginning that the disorganized and undisciplined American fighting men could be trained to fight better than the British – and that they could ultimately defeat the Redcoats. He selected 100 soldiers with leadership potential from the various Colonial militia groups and trained them to be well disciplined fighting men. These 100 men were then returned to their units to in turn train the rest of their men. General von Steuben's methods were highly successful. Even General George Washington was astounded at how this man, although unable to speak English, was able to revive the disheartened troops and make them ready to take on the British. He took a major part in the battle of Yorktown with General Washington. And he was largely responsible for America's defeat of the British in the War for Independence.

10

Early American Yuletide Pickles, Relishes and Sauces

Cabbage Relish –

The Clark Family's Christmas Treat

1 quart green tomatoes	1 quart vinegar
2 quarts cabbage, chopped fine	1 cup sugar
	½ tbls allspice
5 medium onions, chopped fine	¾ tbls mustard seed
	½ tbls celery seed
6 red peppers, chopped fine	2 tbls salt
	2 tsp tumeric

Slice green tomatoes thin and put in small crock. Cover with salted water. Let stand overnight. In the morning, drain, and add chopped cabbage, onions and peppers. Blend mixture nicely. Now pour vinegar into a large kettle. Stir in sugar, allspice, mustard seed, celery seed, salt and tumeric. Lastly, add vegetable mixture to kettle. Bring to quick boil. Immediately put up in pint jars or jelly tumblers and seal with paraffin.

** ** ** ** ** **

Abraham Clark (1726-1794) was a staunch *Bible* believing Christian and New Jersey signer of the *Declaration of Independence.* He was a farmer with very little formal education, a surveyor and a self-taught lawyer. This great patriot fathered 10 children. Two of his two sons were captured by the British and held aboard the notorious *Jersey*, a ship where hundreds of prisoners died while in captivity because of the horrifying conditions. His sons were beaten and tortured in retaliation for what Clark had done. The British authorities offered to release the young men if he would simply refute the American cause. So strong was Abraham Clark's feelings for his country that he courageously refused. Clark strongly opposed the ratification of the *Constitution* until the *Bill of Rights* was made a part of the document.

Bread and Butter Pickles –
Rebecca Motte's Special Recipe

5 medium cucumbers, thinly sliced	1 cup water
3 medium onions, thinly sliced	½ tsp celery seed
	½ tsp mustard seed
¼ cup salt	¾ cup sugar
1 cup vinegar	½ tsp ginger
	¼ tsp tumeric

Combine sliced cucumbers and onions in a small crock. Sprinkle with the salt and set aside for 2 hours. Then drain off liquid and discard. Put the vinegar and water in a kettle and heat to boiling. Stir in the celery seed, mustard seed, sugar, ginger and tumeric. Add cucumbers and onions from the crock. Let cook until cucumbers and onions are tender. Pack while hot in freshly sterilized canning jars and seal.

** ** ** ** **

129

Rebecca was a young church going Christian woman who had sailed from England to wed Jacob Motte, a wealthy South Carolina planter. She was a widow by the time the Revolutionary War began and was forced to abandon her mansion when it was forcibly taken by the British for use as their headquarters. In retaliation, this gutsy patriot purchased a bow from some Indians. She then hired an expert marksman to shoot fire-tipped arrows at her former home and burn it to the ground.

Hollandaise Sauce –

A Favorite of John Quincy Adams

6 tbls lemon juice   Pinch of pepper

Pinch of salt   6 egg yolks, beaten

1 cup butter

Put lemon juice in a saucepan with the salt and pepper. Bring to boil. Continue boiling until liquid is reduced by one-half. Take from stove. Add 3 tablespoons cold water and the beaten egg yolks. Blend thoroughly and put saucepan back on stove. Stir in the butter, a little at a time. *Do not let mixture come to a boil.* If sauce thickens to much, add a little more cold water to stop from curdling. **Note:** *This sauce was a favorite of John Quincy Adams during the Christmas holidays when served over cauliflower and with brook trout and broiled salmon dishes.*

** ** ** ** **

John Quincy Adams (1767-1848), 6th President of the United States, was the son of John Adams, our 2nd President. He was politically active during the administration of President James Monroe and became his Secretary of State. Adams was elected to the Presidency by the House of Representatives in 1825 over Andrew Jackson. He was defeated by Jackson when he ran for re-election in 1828. On July 4th, 1821, Adams, a devout Christian, declared: *"From the day of the Declaration ... they [the American people] were bound by the laws of God, which they all, and by the laws of the Gospel, which they nearly all, acknowledge as the rules of their conduct."*

Ripe Tomato Pickle Relish –
As Made by Alexander Stephens' Mother

4 pints tomatoes, peeled and chopped	6 tbls salt
6 tbls onion, chopped	2 tsp nutmeg
6 tbls red pepper, chopped	1 tsp cloves
6 tbls celery, chopped	1 tsp cinnamon
8 tbls sugar	6 tbls mustard seed
	2 cups vinegar

Put tomatoes, onions, red peppers and celery in a stone crock. Stir in the sugar, salt, nutmeg, cloves, cinnamon, and mustard seed. Lastly add the vinegar. Cover and set aside in a cool place. Let stand at least a week before using. May easily be kept a year.

** ** ** ** **

This simple yet excellent recipe was concocted by the mother of a man who is most often forgotten in our nation's long and glorious history.   Alexander H.

Stephens (1812-83), a devout Christian man, was the Vice-President of the Confederacy in 1861 under the great Jefferson Davis. A brilliant thinker, Stephens was the man behind the drafting of the *Confederate Constitution*. He had previously been a prominent attorney, a Congressman in Georgia from 1843 to 1859, and instrumental in securing passage of the *Kansas Nebraska Act*. As Vice- President of the Confederacy, Stephens worked hard for prisoner exchanges. He also opposed all moves toward centralization of government power and suspension of civil rights during the war. This man again served in Congress from 1873 to 1882 and was Governor of Georgia in 1882.

Apple Chutney –

As Made by Mrs. West for Christmas

15 large sour apples, chopped	1 quart vinegar
2 large onions, chopped	2 cups brown sugar
12 green peppers, chopped	2 tbls ginger
1 cup raisins	2 tbls salt
2 tbls white mustard seed	

Put chopped apples, onions and peppers in a large kettle. Add raisins and vinegar. Blend everything well. Bring to boil and let simmer for 2 hours. Then stir in brown sugar, ginger, salt and mustard seed. Slowly simmer for another hour. Put in glass canning jars and seal while hot. Makes about 5 pints.

** ** ** ** **

Samuel West (1731-1807) holds the unique distinction of being the official Chaplain in the Continental Army during the Revolutionary War. This dedicated Christian patriot was able to greatly help General Washington when he exposed a treasonous letter written to the British Admiral in Newport, Rhode Island, from Dr. Benjamin Church. West was also a member of the Massachusetts Convention that adopted the *United States Constitution*.

Uncooked Pickle Relish –

John Ericsson's Favorite on Christmas

1 peck half-ripe tomatoes	2 quarts vinegar
2 cups celery, chopped	1 pound brown sugar
8 small onions, chopped	1 cup salt
4 green peppers, chopped	4 tbls mustard seed
4 red peppers, chopped	¼ tsp nutmeg, grated

Peel tomatoes and put them through a meat grinder. Drain well. Put them in a stone crock with the chopped celery, onions, green peppers and red peppers. Set aside momentarily. Now blend together in a wooden mixing bowl the vinegar, brown sugar, salt, mustard seed and grated nutmeg. Add this mixture to vegetables in stone crock. Stir thoroughly until well mixed. Cover and let stand 6 weeks before using. It will keep indefinitely.

** ** ** ** **

John Ericsson (1803-89), a devout Christian, was the brilliant Swedish-American inventor of the screw propeller in 1836 that revolutionized water navigation. And in 1837 he built a steam ship with twin screw propellers. Ericsson designed the Union's ironclad *Monitor*. This was the first vessel ever outfitted with a revolving gun turret. After the Confederate ironclad frigate *Merrimac* sunk the *Cumberland,* it had to be withdrawn from battle when going up against the *Monitor* on March 9, 1861. Ericsson was congratulated by Chief Engineer Alban S. Stimers, U.S.N., after its battle with the *Merrimac*: *"Captain Ericsson, I congratulate you on your great success; thousands here this day bless you. I have heard whole crews cheer you; every man feels that you have saved the nation by furnishing us with the means to whip an ironclad frigate that was, until your arrival, having it all her own way with our most powerful vessels."*

Very Thick White Sauce –
As Eaten on Christmas by Joseph Hewes

4 tbls butter, melted   1 cup milk, scalded

4 tbls flour   ½ tsp salt

Pepper to suit taste

Combine butter and flour in small pot and stir until nicely blended. Cook over another pot of hot water (use a double boiler today). Slowly add milk while constantly stirring until mixture in thick and smooth. Add salt and a few grains of pepper. Joseph Hewes especially liked this thick sauce with chicken croquettes or other similar dishes. *Note: To make a thinner white sauce more suitable for preparing cream soups -- simply decrease the butter and flour to 3 tablespoons each and follow same basic instructions.*

** ** ** ** **

Joseph Hewes (1730-1779) of North Carolina, signer of the *Declaration of Independence* was a Quaker and a pacifist. Hewes came under much intense pressure from his church associates, family members and friends not to sign the *Declaration* and not to get involved. He knew he would be hanged if the British were to win the War for American Independence. Yet, after much soul searching, this brave Christian patriot declared: *"My country is entitled to my services, and I shall not shrink from the cause, even though it should cost me my life."* Hewes died at the age of 49, still shunned by his Quaker family and friends.

11

Batter Bread and Other Christmas Corn Meal Favorites

Plain Corn Bread –
A Mason Family Christmas Specialty

1 cup flour	1 tbls sugar
3 tsp baking powder	1 cup corn meal
¼ tsp baking soda	1 egg, beaten
1 tsp salt	1-1/2 cups sour milk

4 tbls shortening, melted

Sift together in a wooden mixing bowl the flour, baking powder, baking soda, salt and sugar. Then stir in the corn meal. Next work in the beaten egg and sour milk. Lastly add the melted shortening. Beat until everything is thoroughly blended. Grease a shallow baking pan. Pour batter into pan. Bake at 425 degrees for about 25 minutes. Cut into 9 squares and serve while hot with butter.

** ** ** ** **

George Mason (1725-92) was an early leader in the cause of freedom in early America. This man was a Virginia planter and close personal friend of George Washington. He was strongly against the unfair taxing policies of the British in the Colonies. Mason, a devout Christian, assisted in developing the *Constitution*, but then ended up opposing its ratification in Virginia. He believed it gave the Federal government too much power and, therefore could take away the rights of the States as well as the citizens.

Batter Bread –

A Christmas Favorite of the Marshalls

1 cup white corn meal	1 tsp butter, melted
1 tsp baking soda, heaping	1-1/2 cups water, scalding
1 tsp salt	1 egg
1-1/2 cups milk	

Sift together in a wooden mixing bowl the white corn meal, baking powder and salt. Add melted butter and blend thoroughly. Pour scalding water over this mixture. Beat in the egg and milk. Pour batter into a shallow buttered baking pan. Stir 2 or 3 times while baking at 350 degrees for 30 to 35 minutes. *Note: This delightful old batter bread "receipt" was a regular Christmas morning breakfast favorite of the Marshall family for a great number of years.*

** ** ** ** **

John Marshall (1755-1835) from Virginia, served as a Captain in the Continental Army under General George Washington. He was at Valley Forge in 1777-1778 during the terrible freezing winter. Marshall strongly advocated that Virginia ratify the *Constitution*. President John Adams appointed Marshall to be the Chief Justice of the United States Supreme Court in 1801. He held this high position for a period of 34 years. Interestingly enough, it was at John Marshall's funeral in 1835 that the Liberty Bell cracked. According to Marshall's daughter, *"he believed in the truth of the Christian Revelation ... of the supreme divinity of our Saviour ... he thought it was his duty to make a public confession of the Saviour."*

Apple Corn Bread –
Mrs. Dickinson's Christmas Specialty

2 cups yellow corn meal	2 tbls butter
¼ cup honey	2 eggs, well beaten
1-1/2 tsp salt	1 tsp baking soda
2 cups sour milk	1 tbls cold water

2 cups apples, chopped fine

Place yellow corn meal, honey, salt, sour milk and butter in upper part of a double boiler. Let cook 12 minutes. Set aside to cool. Then stir in the beaten eggs. Now dissolve baking soda in tablespoon of cold water and add to pot. Lastly add finely chopped apples. Blend everything thoroughly. Set aside momentarily. Grease a 9 x 9-inch baking pan. Pour batter into this. Bake at 425 degrees for 35 to 40 minutes. Serve hot with butter.

** ** ** ** **

John Dickinson (1732-1808) was a member of the Continental Congress from Pennsylvania and a signer of the *Constitution*. This great American patriot met with other delegates less than two months before the signing of the *Declaration of Independence*. He suggested that all members of the Convention subscribe to the following stipulation before being seated: ***"I do profess faith in God the Father, and in Jesus Christ his Eternal Son the true God, and in the Holy Spirit, one God blessed for evermore; and I do acknowledge the Holy Scriptures of the Old and New Testaments to be given by Divine Inspiration."***

Corn Meal Puffs –

A Christmas Favorite of Samuel Adams

2 cups yellow corn meal   1 tsp salt

2 cups water, boiling   8 egg whites, beaten

Put yellow corn meal in a wooden mixing bowl and pour boiling water over it. Add salt. Stir until it is cool. Take stiffly beaten egg whites and carefully fold into corn meal mixture. Set aside momentarily. Grease muffin type tins. Pour mixture into tins. Bake at 425 degrees until lightly browned. Serve at once while steaming hot.

** ** ** ** **

Samuel Adams (1722-1803), another signer of the *Declaration of Independence*, was for more than 20 years before this a defiant anti-British leader and notable patriot in the Colonies. Best known as *"The Father of the American Revolution,"* he called for the first Continental Congress. Adams served as a member of this body until

1781. He wrote that *"the right to freedom"* was *"the gift of the Almighty"* and that *"the rights of the colonists as Christians ... may be best understood by reading and carefully studying ... the New Testament."*

In a Draft Resolution for the Continental Congress dated November 1, 1777, Adams included these words: *"... it may please God through the merits of Jesus Christ ... to afford His blessing on the governments of these States ... to inspire our commanders both by land and sea, and all under them with that wisdom and fortitude which may render them fit instruments, under the Providence of Almighty God, to secure for these United States, the greatest of all human blessings, independence and peace – that it may please Him ... "*

Christmas Corn Sticks –
Winfield Scott Hancock Enjoyed These

½ cup flour	1 cup yellow corn meal
3 tsp baking powder	1 egg, well beaten
½ tsp salt	1 cup milk
2 tbls sugar	2 tbls shortening, melted

Sift together in a wooden mixing bowl the flour, baking powder, salt and sugar. Stir into this the yellow corn meal. Then add beaten egg and milk. Lastly add melted shortening. Blend everything thoroughly. Set aside momentarily. Grease some hot cast iron corn stick baking pans. Pour batter into these pans. Bake at 400 degrees for around 30 to 40 minutes or until lightly browned. Makes 12 small corn sticks.

** ** ** ** **

Winfield Scott Hancock (1824-86) was born in Pennsylvania and graduated from West Point in 1844. He became one of the Union's finest commanding officers. General Hancock was seriously wounded at Gettysburg. Yet, he went on to lead his troops in numerous other battles in such places as the Wilderness and Petersburg. When the Civil War was over, he then conducted a vigorous campaign against the Cheyenne Indians between 1867 and 1868. Hancock, a devout Christian, was a tall, dignified man. He ran for President in 1880 and lost a close campaign race to James Garfield.

Sour Milk Spoon Bread –

The Prescott Family's Christmas Special

2-1/2 cups water	2 egg yolks
2 cups corn meal	1-1/2 cups sour milk
2 tbls shortening, melted	1 tsp baking soda
1-1/2 tsp salt	2 egg whites, beaten

Put water in small kettle and bring to a boil. Gradually add corn meal, stirring constantly so as not to lump. Set aside to cool. Then stir in melted shortening, salt, egg yolks, sour milk and baking soda. Beat mixture for about 2 minutes so everything will be thoroughly blended. Lastly, fold in stiffly beaten egg whites. Grease a baking pan. Pour batter into pan. Bake at 425 degrees for about 40 minutes. Makes enough to feed 6 people.

** ** ** ** **

William Prescott (1726-95) was another of the often forgotten early American Christian patriots who fervently believed in the cause of liberty and freedom. This man was a Colonel during the Revolutionary War who is best remembered for commanding the Colonial Militia at the never to be forgotten Battle of Bunker Hill. When the British blockaded the Boston port on 1774, he wrote this in support of the people: *"Let us all be of one heart, and stand fast in the liberty wherewith Christ has made us free. And may He, of His infinite mercy, grant us deliverance from all our troubles."*

Spider Corn Cake –

A Favorite of the Braxton Bragg Family

4 eggs	4 cups milk
1/2 cup sugar	2 tsp salt
2 tsp baking soda	3-1/3 cups yellow corn meal
2 cups sour milk	2/3 cup flour

4 tbls butter

Cream eggs and sugar in a large wooden mixing bowl. Dissolve baking soda in sour milk. Add this, 2 cups milk and salt to ingredients in mixing bowl. Gradually stir in yellow corn meal and flour so as not to lump. Continue stirring (not beating) until everything is nicely blended. Heat a large cast iron skillet. Melt in the butter. Let butter run up sides of skillet. Pour mixture in skillet and smooth over top. Using a circular pattern, slowly pour last 2 cups milk over entire top of mixture. Do not stir. Place skillet in oven. Be careful not to shake or bump. Bake at 350 degrees for from 20 to 35 minutes.

When done there will be a streak of delicious custard running through the corn cake. Serve while hot with plenty of butter. Makes enough for 2 skillets of Spider Corn Cake.

** ** ** ** **

Braxton Bragg (1817-76), Confederate General, graduated from West Point in 1837 and had a rather distinguished military record early on in his career. He was an advisor to Confederate President Jefferson Davis throughout most of 1864 and joined Davis in his attempt to escape Union forces at the end of the Civil War. But Bragg, a professed Christian, wasn't thought very highly of as a military leader later in his career. Generals E. Kirby Smith and Leonidas Polk both asked Jefferson Davis to relieve Bragg from any command position as early as 1862. General Nathan Bedford Forrest contemptuously cursed Bragg. A soldier's diary, written in 1863, had this to offer: *"General Bragg is not fit for a general ... I believe he is a coward ... "* Dr. D.W. Yandell, an army surgeon, wrote: *"General Bragg is either stark mad or utterly incompetent."*

12

Homemade Bread and Rolls for an Old-Fashioned Christmas

Meat Bread –

A Favorite of the Randolph Family

1 yeast cake	8 cups flour
1 cup warm water	1 pound beef, ground

Salt to suit taste

Make a ferment by crumbling the yeast cake in the cup of warm water. Add enough flour to make a thin batter. Put the rest of the flour into a large pan. Add the ground beef. Blend thoroughly. Make a hollow place in the middle. Pour the ferment in the hollow. Sprinkle a little flour over the top. Cover pan with a towel. Put in warm place for ½ hour to rise. When ferment has risen (when flour sprinkled over top begins to crack), add sufficient warm water as necessary to work mixture into a smooth, compact dough. Add salt to suit taste. Knead and form dough into loaves. Place in well-greased bread pans. Cover and set aside in warm place. Let rise for about 1 hour. Bake immediately at 450 degrees for 45 minutes or until done. Test for doneness with a toothpick. Makes 2 large loaves.

** ** ** ** **

Edmund Jennings Randolph (1753-1813), a Virginian, served in the Continental Army under George Washington during the American War for Independence. This devout Christian patriot was later a member of the Continental Congress as well as a delegate to the Constitutional Convention. Randolph was the man who proposed that each session of Congress be opened in the morning with prayer. He also served his country as its first Attorney General and its second Secretary of State. Randolph played a major role in developing the *Constitution*, yet he refused to sign it and initially opposed its adoption. However, he later greatly assisted in getting this historic document ratified by Virginia.

Date-Nut Bread Loaf –
The Vallandigham Family Recipe

1-1/2 cups flour	1-1/2 cups milk
5 tsp baking powder	¼ cup molasses
1-1/2 tsp salt	1-1/2 cups graham flour
¼ tsp baking soda	1 cup dates, chopped,
½ cup brown sugar	dredged in graham flour

1 cup walnuts, chopped

Sift together in a wooden mixing bowl the flour, baking powder, salt and baking soda. Stir in brown sugar, milk and molasses. Add graham flour, dredged dates and chopped walnuts. Beat all ingredients thoroughly until nicely blended. Grease a loaf pan. Pour batter into loaf pan. Bake at 375 degrees for 1 hour.

** ** ** ** **

Clement Laird Vallandigham (1820-71), a Christian journalist, lawyer and Ohio political figure, was openly sympathetic to the Confederate cause during the Civil War. For this he was accused of being a traitor. He was arrested and charged with *"treasonable conduct."* President Lincoln ordered him banished to the South after he was convicted of treason in 1863 for defiantly speaking out against the war, an act prohibited by law at that time. Vallandigham courageously re-entered the North and vigorously worked against Lincoln during his re-election campaign of 1864. He strongly opposed the vengeful Reconstruction policies of the Radical Republicans but was largely unsuccessful in doing much to stop the Northerners from pushing through their hate-filled anti-Southern legislation.

Corn Meal Rolls –

A Pinckney Family Christmas Favorite

1-1/4 cup flour	1 tbls sugar
¾ cup corn meal	2 tbls butter
3 tsp baking powder	1 egg
1 tsp salt	½ cup milk

Sift together in a wooden mixing bowl the flour, corn meal, baking powder, salt and sugar. Cut in the butter with a fork. Beat egg and milk together in a separate bowl. Then add this to dry ingredients in first bowl. Work together until a soft dough is formed. Toss and knead a little and then roll out on a floured board. Shape into rolls. Place on greased baking tin. Bake at 425 degrees for 12 to 15 minutes. *Note: The Pinckneys sometimes made their rolls with rye flour and corn meal.*

** ** ** ** **

Charles Cotesworth Pinckney (1746-1825), was one of three brothers who came from a prominent Christian family in South Carolina. Each brother gained a measure of fame during the Revolutionary War and thereafter. Charles Cotesworth was a Brigadier General who had studied for a military career at the prestigious Royal Military Academy of France. A wealthy planter in civilian life, he became General George Washington's aide-de-camp. Pinckney was a delegate to the Constitutional Convention. He turned down President Washington's offers of various cabinet positions as well as an appointment on the United States Supreme Court. Pinckney once declared: *"Blasphemy against the Almighty is denying His being ... it is punished ... by fine and imprisonment, for Christianity is part of the laws of the land."*

Steamed Rye Can Bread –

As Made by the Gatling Family

1 cup rye flour	1 tsp baking soda
1 cup corn meal	½ cup raisins
1 cup graham flour	2 cups water
1 tsp salt	¾ cup molasses

Combine in a wooden mixing bowl the rye flour, corn meal, graham flour, salt and baking soda. Then stir in the raisins. Add water and molasses. Blend everything thoroughly. Grease some 1 pound cans. Fill each can 2/3 full of batter. Cover tightly. Steam for 2 hours. Take bread from cans and slice. Serve while hot with butter.

** ** ** ** **

Richard Jordan Gatling (1818-1903), a North Carolina physician and a professed Christian, patented his revolving 6-barrel hand cranked Gatling machine gun on November 4, 1862. But President Lincoln initially ignored this new weapon's military potential because Gatling was suspected of having Confederate sympathies. His new weapon could fire an astounding 250 rounds a minute. A few of these rapid fire guns were first tried aboard Union ships during the Siege of Petersburg. Union General Benjamin Franklin Butler later used 12 of the guns in Virginia campaigns. The United States Army finally officially adopted the Gatling gun in 1866. Dr. Gatling sincerely believed that wars would cease to exist in the future because off the devastating weapon he had created.

Steamed Molasses Can Bread –
As Mrs. Wythe Served it to Her Family

1 cup flour	1 cup corn meal
1-1/3 tsp baking soda	1 cup graham flour
1 tsp salt	2 cups sour milk
1 tsp baking powder	¾ cup molasses

Sift together in a wooden mixing bowl the flour, baking soda, salt and baking powder. Add corn meal and graham flour. Blend all ingredients well. In a separate bowl, combine sour milk and molasses. Add this to dry ingredients in first bowl and stir well. Grease some 1 pound cans. Fill each can 2/3 full with batter. Cover tightly. Steam for 3 hours. Take bread from cans and slice. Serve while hot with butter.

** ** ** ** **

George Wythe (1726-1806) from Virginia, was one of the 56 heroic signers of the *Declaration of*

Independence. He was also a member of the Continental Congress. Wythe established the first law professorship in the United States at William and Mary College and taught such great American patriots as Thomas Jefferson, Henry Clay and John Marshall. This man freed his slaves in his will and left his entire library to Jefferson. He died before his time due to arsenic poisoning by a greedy grand nephew who was impatiently waiting for his inheritance. In February of 1776, Wythe, a devout Christian, helped John Adams and Robert Sherman write instructions for an embassy to be opened in Canada. He wrote this: *"You are further to declare ... that ... the right to hold office was to be extended to persons of any Christian denomination."*

Cracked Wheat Bread –
Eaten on Christmas by the Chase Family

2 yeast cakes	2 cups water, boiling
2/3 cup water, lukewarm	1 tsp salt
½ cup honey	2 tbls butter, melted
1-1/2 cups cracked wheat	2-1/2 cups gluten flour
3 cups whole wheat flour	

Crumble yeast cakes in a small bowl with the lukewarm water. When dissolved, stir in 2 tablespoons honey and 2 tablespoons flour. Blend well and set aside momentarily to let yeast get thick and bubbly. Meanwhile, put cracked wheat in large wooden mixing bowl. Pour boiling water over this. Then stir in the rest of the honey, salt and melted butter. Add bubbly yeast mixture to this and thoroughly blend. Gradually add gluten flour and whole wheat flour. Knead for minimum of 10 minutes until dough is smooth and elastic. Place in well-greased bowl. Cover with towel or blanket. Set in warm place, free from drafts, to rise until light – about 1 hour. When dough has risen, punch down with fist. Again cover with towel or blanket and let rise once more – about 30 minutes this time. Punch dough down again. Knead for a few minutes. Form into 3 loaves. Place in well-greased bread pans. Cover and let rise again – about 1 hour. Bake at 350 degrees for about 1 hour. Test for doneness with a toothpick.

** ** ** ** **

Samuel Chase (1741-1811), son of an Anglican clergyman, was born in a farmhouse in Maryland. His mother died during or soon after his birth. He was appointed as an Associate Justice on the United States Supreme Court by President George Washington. This is where he achieved his greatest fame amid much controversy. Impeachment proceedings were brought against him in 1805, but he was acquitted by Congress. Chase was a fervid Colonial revolutionary who bravely signed the *Declaration of Independence*. His fiercely independent nature, outspokenness and stormy disposition combined with great oratorical skills brought him the label of the "Demosthenes of Maryland." This man once said: ***"By our form of government, the Christian religion is the established religion; and all sects and denominations of Christians are placed upon the same equal footing, and are equally entitled to protection in their religious liberty."***

Dinner Graham Rolls –
The Butler Family's Christmas Treat

3 cups graham flour   2 tbls sugar

2 cups flour   1 tsp salt

1-1/2 cups milk

Take a large wooden mixing bowl and blend all of the above ingredients. Work with the hands until a smooth dough is achieved. Grease a square, shallow cake pan. Now form dough into a number of elongated rolls. Lay them, just touching, in pan. Brush over rolls with coating of milk. Bake at 350 degrees for 20 to 25 minutes. When removing from oven, rub each roll with a little butter. Serve while hot.

** ** ** ** **

Benjamin Franklin Butler (1818-93) became Governor of New Orleans in May of 1862. He was evidently a dictatorial, extremely corrupt, and power mad individual. Butler ordered a man hanged for merely taking down a Union flag. And he issued what was known at the time as his ridiculous *"Woman Order."* This so called Butler's law declared that any female caught insulting a Union military man would be treated and punished as a prostitute. His many notorious actions created international protests and he was eventually removed from office in December of 1862. Butler, a man who professed himself a Christian, had many friends in high places and subsequently became a Major General

163

in the Union Army. He led a military force in 1865 under orders to capture Fort Fisher on the coast of North Carolina. The mission failed due to Butler's incompetence as a military leader. As a consequence, he was relieved of his command. Butler was considered to be a typically worthless politically appointee -- a high ranking officer who was of dubious value to the Union cause.

13

Drop Biscuits, Berry Muffins and Other Christmas Specialties

Rich Cream Biscuits –

Mrs. Roger Sherman's Christmas Best

2 cups flour	½ tsp salt
3 tbls baking powder	4 tbls butter

¾ cup cream

Sift together in a wooden mixing bowl the flour, baking powder and salt. Blend in the butter with a fork or the finger tips. The mixture should resemble coarse corn meal. Lastly, stir in cream, again using a fork. Turn out dough onto lightly floured board. Knead for about 30 seconds. Then roll out to ½ inch thick sheet. Cut with floured biscuit cutter or appropriate size upside down drinking glass. Place on ungreased baking sheet. Bake at 450 degrees for 12 to 15 minutes. Yield is 12 to 16 biscuits.

** ** ** ** **

Roger Sherman (1721-93) was a well-known patriot in the Colonies before and during and after the Revolutionary War period of our history. He is the only one of the Founding Fathers to have signed all four of the major founding documents. These were: 1774 – *Articles of Association*; 1776 – *Declaration of Independence*; 1777 – *Articles of Confederation*; 1787 – *Constitution of the United States.* Sherman was a member of the Continental Congress and made an astounding 138 speeches at the Constitutional Convention. He was also the man who seconded the motion made by Benjamin Franklin that Congress be opened each day with a prayer.

Berry Muffins –

A Velazquez Christmas Favorite

½ cup sugar   3 tsp baking powder

4 tbls shortening   ½ tsp salt

3 egg yolks   2/3 cup milk

2-1/2 cups flour   1 cup blackberries

3 egg whites, stiffly beaten

Put sugar, shortening and egg yolks in a wooden mixing bowl. Cream together until light. Sift together in a separate mixing bowl the flour, baking powder and salt. Add these dry ingredients, alternately, with the milk, to the mixture in first bowl. Beat until smooth. Stir in the blackberries. Lastly, fold in stiffly beaten egg whites. Put mixture in well-greased muffin tins. Bake at 425 degrees for about 25 minutes. Serve while hot.

** ** ** ** **

Lieutenant Harry Buford (Loreta Janeta Velazquez) (1842?-97), a spirited young Catholic girl, was born in Cuba to an aristocratic Spanish family. She came to the United States and was educated in New Orleans. Loreta met and fell in love with a young Confederate army officer. She was but 16 when they married in 1856, against the wishes of her family. A fiercely independent young lady, Loreta proceeded to join the army along with her husband while disguised as a man. She went under the fictitious name of Harry Buford. Loreta's husband was killed early in the Civil War, but Loreta stayed in the army and fought at First Bull Run and Fort Donelson. This heroic Christian patriot was eventually exposed as a woman in 1863. Yet, she continued to work for the Confederacy as a spy behind Union lines. She later wrote and published a book in 1876 called *The Woman in Battle*.

Walnut Muffins –
As Made for John S. Mosby

1/3 cup sugar	4 tsp baking powder
¼ cup shortening	½ tsp salt
2 eggs	½ cup walnuts, chopped
2-1/2 cups flour	¾ cup milk

Cream the sugar and shortening in a wooden mixing bowl. Add eggs, one at a time, beating thoroughly, while adding. In a separate mixing bowl, sift together the flour, baking powder and salt. Add this and chopped walnuts, alternately, with milk, to mixture in first bowl. Beat everything together until smooth. Put into well-greased muffin tins. Bake at 375 degrees for about 25 minutes. Serve while hot with butter.

** ** ** ** **

John Singleton Mosby (1833-1916) was a widely known, heroic and dashing young Christian cavalry officer who courageously fought for the Confederacy. On March 9, 1863, he pulled off one of his more daring exploits in Virginia, only 20 miles from Washington. Mosby and 29 of his men raided the Union camp at Fairfax Court House and captured General Edwin Stoughton, two captains, 30 soldiers and 58 horses. Not one of his cavalrymen was killed or even wounded during this escapade. So elusive was Mosby during the Civil War that he became known as *"The Gray Ghost."*

Captain Mosby's deeds earned him an awesome reputation as fearless man of action. So dangerous were he and his raiders to the Union cause that General Grant once gave orders that he be hanged if captured. They later became friends after the Civil War was over and Mosby became one of Grant's major supporters when he campaigned for the Presidency.

Sour Cream Biscuits –

Christmas Favorites of the Clark Family

2 cups flour	3 tsp baking powder
½ tsp salt	½ tsp baking soda

½ cup sour cream

Sift some flour into a wooden mixing bowl. Measure out 2 cups. Sift into another mixing bowl this flour with the salt, baking powder and baking soda. Add sour cream. Mix to the consistency of a nice roll out dough. Add 1 teaspoon water if dough is not soft enough. Turn dough out onto lightly floured board. Knead lightly. Pat or roll out into ½ inch thick sheet. Cut with floured biscuit cutter or upside down drinking glass. Place biscuits on a well-greased baking tin. Bake at 450 degrees for about 12 minutes. Serve while hot with butter and jam or jelly. Makes 12 nice biscuits.

** ** ** ** **

George Rogers Clark (1752-1818) was a renown military leader on the American frontier. This man moved to Kentucky in 1775 and organized a militia there during the Revolutionary War. He began attacking British outposts in Illinois with less than 200 men. An unwavering Christian leader, Clark's successes there brought the French inhabitants in the area over to his side in the war. After the British General Henry Hamilton occupied Vincennes in December of 1778, Clark counter-attacked during the harsh winter in February of 1779 with a small group of his soldiers. Marching for 18 days through icy water, often with little or no food, his men defeated the British and took General Hamilton prisoner. The British General was later to say that Clark's military feat was *"unequalled perhaps in history."*

Rich Baking Powder Biscuits –
As Eaten by Thomas Heyward

3 cups flour   1 tsp salt

4 tsp baking powder   6 tbls butter

1 cup cream

Sift some flour into a wooden mixing bowl. Measure out 3 cups. Sift into another mixing bowl this flour with the baking powder and salt. Cut in butter with a fork or using fingers. Add cream and work this into a nice dough. Turn out onto lightly floured board. Pat or roll out into ½ inch thick sheet. Cut with floured biscuit cutter or upside down drinking glass. Place biscuits on well-greased baking tin. Bake at 450 degrees for about 12 minutes. Serve while hot. Makes 16 biscuits.

** ** ** ** **

Thomas Heyward, Jr. (1746-1809), the eldest son of one of South Carolina's wealthiest planters, was another heroic Christian signer of the *Declaration of Independence*. While a member of the Continental Congress from 1776 to 1778, he also signed the *Articles of Confederation*. Heyward was wounded in 1779 while fighting the British on Port Royal Island along the South Carolina coast near his home. In 1780, the British destroyed Heyward's Whitehall Plantation and carried off all of the slaves. This great patriot was captured in 1780 during the battle defending Charleston. He was offered amnesty by the British if he would repudiate the

American cause. Heyward defiantly refused. Yes, Thomas Heyward paid dearly for his love of country. He never saw his wife again. She died while he was imprisoned in the Crown stockade at St. Augustine, Florida. Heyward was finally given his freedom in July of 1781. Shortly before he was released by the British, this man celebrated Independence Day by rewriting the British national anthem, "God Save the King," to "God Save the Thirteen States." This became the rallying song that echoed from New Hampshire to Georgia. When Thomas Heyward died at the age of 62, he was buried in the family cemetery at Old House Plantation.

Whole Wheat Muffins –
As Beecher Liked Them for Breakfast

2 cups whole wheat flour	½ tsp salt
1 tsp baking powder	2 tbls butter, melted
1 tsp baking soda	1 egg
2 tbls sugar	1-1/2 cups sour milk

Mix but do not sift in a wooden bowl the whole wheat flour, baking powder, baking soda, sugar and salt. Stir in the melted butter, unbeaten egg and sour milk. Beat only enough to make a smooth, lump-free batter. Lightly grease a muffin tin. Fill 2/3 full. Bake at 425 degrees for about 25 minutes. Makes 12 nice muffins.

** ** ** ** **

Henry Ward Beecher (1813-1887) was an outspoken opponent of slavery and the brother of Harriet Beecher Stowe, the author of *Uncle Tom's Cabin.* Beecher was behind the shipping of carbines to anti-slavery

175

proponents in boxes labeled *"Bibles."* These rifles were called *"Beecher's Bibles."* Why? Because this well known Protestant minister had publicly stated that there was *"more moral power in one of those instruments so far as the slaveholders were concerned than in 100 Bibles."* Beecher once said this: *"The Bible is God's chart for you to steer by, to keep you from the bottom of the sea, and to show you where the harbor is, and how to reach it without running on the rocks or bars."*

Christmas Drop Biscuits –
Abner Doubleday's Favorite

2-3/4 cups flour   1 tsp salt

4 tsp baking powder   6 tbls butter

1-1/4 cup milk

Sift together in a wooden mixing bowl the flour, baking powder and salt. Rub in butter with fingers until mixture resembles corn meal. Add milk. Stir sufficiently to blend everything thoroughly. Set aside momentarily. Grease a large baking sheet. Drop batter by tablespoonfuls onto baking sheet. Bake at 425 degrees for 10 to 15 minutes. Serve while hot with butter.

** ** ** ** **

Abner Doubleday (1819-93), a New York native, graduated from West Point and was involved militarily in both the Mexican and the Seminole Wars. Doubleday was the man who, while on garrison duty, actually fired the first shot from Fort Sumter. He also fought gallantly in the Shenandoah Campaign and won regular, well deserved promotions. This fine soldier also saw action at such places as Second Bull Run, Antietam and Fredericksburg. Major General Doubleday, who was raised by a stalwart Christian family, was given temporary command of I Corps when General John Reynolds was killed during the Battle of Gettysburg in 1863. This is the same man who was to later become famous as the founder of America's national pastime – baseball. He is widely credited with inventing the game in 1839 although some sport's authorities and historians dispute this.

14

Delicious Christmas Cakes from Long, Long Ago

Unique Christmas Layer Cake –
A Recipe Handed Down by Mrs. Wayne

½ cup butter	1 tsp salt
1-1/2 cups sugar	1 cup milk
2-1/2 cups flour	1 tbls lemon juice
2 tsp baking powder	4 egg whites, beaten

Cream the butter and sugar in a large wooden mixing bowl. In a separate mixing bowl sift together the flour, baking powder and salt. Add these dry ingredients to first bowl, alternately, with the milk. Blend everything thoroughly. Then stir in the lemon juice. Lastly, fold in the stiffly beaten egg whites. Set aside momentarily. Grease two round 9-inch cake pans. Dust with a coating of flour. Now pour cake batter in equal amounts into each pan. Bake at 350 degrees for about 1 hour. Test with toothpick for doneness. Set aside to cool. When cooled, spread *Mrs. Wayne's Christmas Cake Filling* between the layers. Ice with *Mrs. Wayne's Special Boiled Icing*.

Mrs. Wayne's Christmas Cake Filling

¾ cup almonds, chopped	1 cup cherries, chopped
¾ cups raisins, chopped	¼ cup icing

Mix together in a wooden mixing bowl the chopped almonds, raisins and cherries. Add some of the icing from that as prepared below. Blend thoroughly.

Mrs. Wayne's Special Boiled Icing

4 cups sugar	2/3 cup light corn syrup
2/3 cup water	4 egg whites, beaten stiff
	2 tsp vanilla

Put sugar and water in a small kettle. Stir until sugar is completely dissolved. Now add the corn syrup and blend thoroughly. Bring mixture to a boil and cook until syrup forms a soft ball when dropped in cold water. Pour this syrup over stiffly beaten egg whites. Beat constantly until mixture holds its shape. Lastly stir in the vanilla.

** ** ** ** **

Anthony Wayne (1745-96), a man with strong Christian convictions, was a famous commander during the Revolutionary War. He became best known as "Mad

Anthony" due to his fearsome recklessness in battle. General Wayne was instrumental in stopping the Indian uprisings in the West in 1794 and 1795. This man was the hero of the storming and subsequent capture of Stony Point on July 15, 1779.

Rich Steamed Fruit Cake –

Mrs. Rosecrans Christmas Best

6 cups raisins	6 eggs
½ cup dried apples, marmalade	½ cup orange
diced	½ cup grape jelly
½ cup dried cherries, diced	½ square unsweetened chocolate, melted
½ cup dried apricots, diced	2-1/2 cups flour
	1-1/2 tsp baking powder
½ cup figs, chopped	¼ tsp salt
1 cup brandy	¼ tsp allspice
1 cup butter	¼ tsp nutmeg
1-1/2 cups brown sugar	2 tsp cinnamon
2 cups almonds, chopped	2 cups pecans, cut in half

Put raisins, apples, cherries, apricots and figs into a large bowl. Pour in brandy (or grape juice) and let soak overnight. Start the next morning by putting butter and brown sugar in a large wooden mixing bowl. Beat until they are nicely creamed. Then add eggs, one at a time, beating mixture thoroughly. Stir in the orange marmalade, grape jelly and melted chocolate. In a separate mixing bowl, sift together half the flour with the baking powder, salt, allspice, nutmeg and cinnamon. Stir this into the mixture in the first bowl. Sift the rest of the flour over the soaked fruit. Stir well to blend nicely. Now add this to the batter in the first bowl. Lastly stir in the chopped almonds and halved pecans. Place in loaf pans lined with well-greased brown paper. Cover tightly. Set in larger pan of water in oven and let steam slowly for 6 hours. Then uncover and bake at 250 degrees for about 1 hour. Makes 3 nice fruit cakes.

** ** ** ** **

William Starke Rosecrans (1819-98), a Christian, came from a family with outstanding credentials. He was the great grandson of another well known Christian leader in early America, Stephen Hopkins, Colonial Governor of Rhode Island and a signer of the *Declaration of Independence*. Rosecrans graduated from West Point in 1842 with such later to become famous classmates as General James Longstreet and General Abner Doubleday, who was credited with the founding of America's pastime – baseball. When the Civil War broke out, Rosecrans became commanding officer of the 23rd Ohio Volunteer Infantry, which had among its members future

Presidents Rutherford Hayes and William McKinley. Rosecrans soon became a Brigadier General in the Union Army and won an early victory when he defeated Robert E. Lee at Rich Mountain, Virginia. On October 24, 1882, he took command of the Army of the Cumberland. Rosecrans, fondly nicknamed "Old Rosie," was highly regarded as a military strategist by those who knew him best.

Christmas Pound Cake –
As Mrs. Hart Made it for Her Family

1 cup butter	2 tsp baking powder
1 cup powdered sugar	1 tsp vanilla
4 eggs	¾ cup apples, chopped
2 cups flour	¾ cup raisins

1-1/2 cups almonds, chopped

Put the butter and powdered sugar in a large wooden mixing bowl. Beat together until they are nicely creamed. Then add eggs, one at a time, beating mixture thoroughly. Sift together in a separate mixing bowl the flour and baking powder. Stir this in with ingredients in first bowl. Add vanilla, chopped apples, raisins and chopped almonds. Blend everything well. Set aside momentarily. Grease one large or two small loaf pans. Bake at 325 degrees for about 1 hour. *Note: Many young girls in the Colonies were prone to slipping a small piece of cake under their pillow on Christmas eve just prior to going to sleep. This was believed to make her dream of her future husband.*

** ** ** ** **

John Hart (1711-1779), a New Jersey signer of the *Declaration of Independence*, suffered a great deal of hardship as a result of his heroic action. This great Christian patriot was driven from his dying wife's bedside by the vengeful British.. They destroyed his

185

mills and his farm. Hart was forced to live in the woods and hills and hide in caves surrounding the Sourland Mountains for more than a year in order to hide from the Redcoats. He was able to finally return home following American victories at Princeton and Trenton, but only to find that everyone had vanished. His wife had died and all of his 13 children had fled for their lives, never to be seen again. The exhausted man died of a broken heart shortly thereafter on his Hopewell farm.

Coffee Loaf Cake –

Mrs. Hooker's Special Christmas Treat

¾ cup butter	½ tsp mace
2-1/4 cups brown sugar	½ tsp cinnamon
3 ounces chocolate, melted	½ tsp salt
3 cups flour	1 cup strong coffee,
4 tsp baking powder	black and cold

4 eggs

Put the butter and brown sugar in a large wooden mixing bowl. Beat together until they are nicely creamed. Stir in the melted chocolate. Sift together in a separate mixing bowl the flour, baking powder, mace, cinnamon and salt. Stir this in with ingredients in first bowl, alternately, with cold coffee. Drop in eggs, one at a time, beating each in thoroughly. Set aside momentarily. Grease and lightly flour a large loaf pan. Put mixture in pan. Bake at 350 degrees for about 50 minutes. When done, let cake cool in pan. Then turn out on plate. Cover entire cake with special coffee frosting as made below.

Mrs. Hooker's Special Coffee Frosting Recipe

1 cup black coffee,	Powdered sugar
very strong	as required
1 tbls vanilla	2 cups walnuts, chopped

Put the cold black coffee and vanilla in a wooden mixing bowl. Beat in enough powered sugar until mixture becomes stiff enough to spread. Spread liberally on top and sides of cake. Sprinkle top of cake thickly with chopped walnuts.

** ** ** ** **

Joseph Hooker (1814-79) graduated from West Point in the class of 1837 that also included future Civil War Generals Braxton Bragg, Jubal Early and John Sedgwick. Major General Hooker was a tall, handsome and outspoken Christian who often stepped on the toes of his senior officers with his biting criticism. A boastful fellow, he once said: *"May God have mercy on General Lee, for I will have none."* He was subsequently defeated by General Robert E. Lee at Chancellorsville in May of 1863. Hooker, never without his *Bible*, later went on to defeat Confederate General Braxton Bragg at the Battle of Lookout Mountain in Chattanooga, Tennessee, on November 24 of that same year. He was aptly called "Fightin' Joe" as a result of his many daring exploits on the battlefield during the Civil War.

Early American Sponge Cake –
An Ethan Allen Christmas Favorite

4 egg yolks	1 cup sugar
3 tbls cold water	1 cup flour
1 tsp lemon juice	1 tsp baking powder
4 egg whites, well beaten	

Put egg yolks in a wooden mixing bowl and beat until thickened. Stir in cold water and lemon juice. Add sugar. Sift together into this mixture the flour and baking powder. Blend everything thoroughly. Lastly, carefully fold in the fluffy beaten egg whites. Grease a small baking pan. Pour batter into pan. Bake at 350 degrees for 45 minutes. After cake has cooled, cover generously with whipped cream, crushed strawberries and ground walnuts.

** ** ** ** **

Ethan Allen (1737-89) and his five companies of Green Mountain Boys became immediate heroes in the Colonies when they soundly thrashed the British at Fort Ticonderoga in 1775. Not a man to mince his words, Allen called for the surrender of the fort, *"in the name of the Great Jehovah and the Continental Congress."* Flamboyant and sword waving, this hot headed Vermont farmer quickly became everybody's idol. This six-foot brawler had a reputation for strangling wildcats with his bare hands. He became a living legend throughout the Colonies. A patriot and a Christian of the first order, Allen once said: *"Ever since I arrived to a state of manhood, I have felt a sincere passion for liberty."*

Applesauce Cake –
The Forrest Family Christmas Favorite

1 cup shortening	2 tsp nutmeg
2 cups brown sugar	3 tsp cinnamon
2-1/3 cups apple sauce	1 tsp mace
2/3 cup molasses	1 tsp allspice
4 eggs, well beaten	1 tsp cloves
6 tbls lemon juice	2 pounds raisins
4 cups flour	1 cup whole wheat flour
4 tsp baking soda	1 pound apples, sliced thin
1-3/4 tsp salt	1 cup walnuts, chopped

Put shortening and brown sugar in large wooden mixing bowl. Beat together until they are nicely creamed. Stir in the apple sauce, molasses, beaten eggs and lemon juice. Blend well. In a separate bowl, sift some flour and take out 4 cups. Sift these 4 cups again

191

with the baking soda, salt, nutmeg, cinnamon, mace, allspice and cloves. Add this gradually to batter in first bowl and beat thoroughly. Dredge raisins in the whole wheat flour. Now add raisins to mixture. Put a thin layer of batter in paper-lined baking pan. Cover with a layer of sliced apples and chopped walnuts. Cover with another layer of batter. Repeat with sliced apples and chopped nuts. The last layer should be of batter. Bake at 300 to 325 degrees for about 2 hours.

** ** ** ** **

The name of General Nathan Bedford Forrest (1821-77) became so famous during the Civil War that it symbolized the entire Confederate cause. The Union decided that this heroic Southern leader must at all costs be stopped. Forrest, brought up in a fundamental Christian home, was without doubt one of the most outstanding cavalry leaders in the entire war. He was seriously wounded in April of 1862. But Forrest recovered and went on to a phenomenal military career that would bring him fame as probably the greatest, most aggressive, and best known cavalry raider of the Civil War. So feared was Forrest that General Sherman swore to stop him even *"if it costs ten thousand lives and bankrupts the federal treasury."* But even Sherman had little success in this regard.

Soft Fruit Cake –

A Favorite of the Johnston Family

2/3 cup dried apricots, chopped	3 eggs, well beaten
1 cup dried apple slices, chopped	¾ cup milk
	2-1/4 cups flour
1 cup prunes, chopped	1 tsp baking soda
1 cup dried figs, chopped	1 tsp nutmeg
1 cup raisins	½ tsp cloves
2-1/4 cups sugar	½ tsp cinnamon
¾ cup water	3 tsp baking powder
¾ cup butter	1 tsp salt
½ cup peanut butter	2 tbls orange peel, shredded

2 tsp vanilla

Put into a kettle the chopped apricots, apple slices, prunes, figs and raisins. Add ½ cup sugar and water. Stir together and bring to boil. Cover and let simmer 10

193

minutes. Take kettle from stove. Drain off liquid and discard. Set fruit mixture aside to cool. Put remaining 1-3/4 cups sugar and butter in a wooden mixing bowl and beat until creamy. Add peanut butter and mix well. Blend in beaten eggs and milk. Sift some flour in a separate bowl. Measure out 2-1/4 cups. Sift this again (into the first bowl) with the baking soda, nutmeg, cloves, cinnamon, baking powder and salt. Add the fruits from the kettle. Blend everything thoroughly. Lastly stir in shredded orange peel and vanilla. Line a large tube pan with oiled paper. Pour mixture into pan. Bake at 325 degrees for 1 hour. Reduce temperature to 250 degrees and continue baking 30 minutes more.

** ** ** ** **

Albert Sidney Johnston (1803-62), one of the foremost Confederate Generals, graduated from West Point in 1826. He fought honorably in the Black Hawk War, resigned from the U.S. Army in 1834, and became commander of the Texas Army in 1837. Johnston, a devout Christian from his childhood, turned down a Union offer to be General Winfield Scott's second in command. He instead chose to fight on the side of the South and became a full General in the Confederate cause. Jefferson Davis, President of the Confederacy, regarded Johnston to be *"the greatest soldier ... then living."* Johnston was able to defeat the Union forces at Bowling Green, but then suffered losses at Logan Cross Roads, Fort Henry and Fort Donelson. He suffered a serious leg wound at Shiloh on April 6, 1862, the first day of fighting, and subsequently died as a result of his injury. His loss was called *"irreparable"* by Jefferson Davis.

15

Mincemeat Cookies and Other Old-Timey Christmas Treats

Mincemeat Christmas Cookies – The Way Mrs. Hopkins' Made Them

1 cup butter	1/8 tsp ginger
2 cups sugar	1 tsp nutmeg
3 eggs, well beaten	1 tsp baking soda
3 cups flour	1 tsp cloves
1 cup mincemeat	½ tsp salt
1 cup walnuts, chopped	

Cream the butter and sugar in a large wooden mixing bowl until it is light and fluffy. Stir in beaten eggs and enough flour to prevent mixture from curdling. Add mincemeat and mix well. Sift together in a separate bowl the rest of the flour, ginger, nutmeg, baking soda, cloves and salt. When finished, blend these ingredients and the chopped walnuts to the mixture in the first bowl. The cookie mixture should be almost stiff enough to roll. Drop from a teaspoon onto a greased baking pan. Keep them at least 2 inches apart to allow room to spread. Bake at 375 degrees for about 10 minutes. Makes about 4 dozen 2-1/2 inch cookies.

** ** ** ** **

Stephen Hopkins (1707-85) of Rhode Island, afflicted with palsy, was the second oldest signer of the *Declaration of Independence*. After this great Christian patriot affixed his signature to the historic document, he handed the quill to William Ellery. Hopkins spoke: ***"My hands tremble, but my heart does not."*** Stephen Hopkins was a man of unquestionable courage who never doubted the rightness of the quest for American independence. He stood tall and unwavering for liberty and freedom when it counted the most.

Christmas Gingersnaps –
A Livingston Family Favorite

2/3 cup butter	2 tbls ice water
½ cup sugar	4-1/2 cups flour
1 egg, well beaten	1 tbls baking soda
1 cup molasses	1 tbls ginger
1 tbls vinegar	1 tbls cinnamon

Cream butter and sugar together in a large wooden mixing bowl. Then blend in the beaten egg, molasses, vinegar and ice water. Setting this aside momentarily, sift flour, baking soda, ginger and cinnamon together in a separate mixing bowl. Stir into the first bowl as much of this flour blend as possible. Knead in what ever is left of the flour mixture. When finished, place dough on floured board and roll out to a 1/8 inch thick sheet. Sprinkle with sugar. Cut into small 2 to 3 inch round cookies with lightly floured cookie cutter or upside down drinking glass. Lay cookies on lightly buttered baking sheets. Bake at 350 degrees for 10 to 12 minutes. Makes about 6 dozen gingersnaps.

** ** ** ** **

Philip Livingston (1716-78) was a heroic New York signer of the *Declaration of Independence*. This brave man, a Christian, lost most of his business property, his two homes, and his family as a result of his unselfish activities in the cause for his dream of a new America, an

America free of British tyranny. He died a heartbroken man soon thereafter in 1878 while still separated from his family by the war. So strong were his convictions that Philip Livingston risked everything he had in this life for the American Revolution – for the freedom and liberty we still have today in our country.

Walnut Macaroons –

As Eaten by Richard Stockton

2 egg whites   1 cup powdered sugar

1 tbls flour   1 cup walnuts

Beat egg whites until stiff peaks form when beater is taken out. Sift together in a small mixing bowl the flour and powdered sugar. Fold gradually into the beaten egg whites. Reserve 30 walnut halves to use later for a garnish. Crush the remainder of the walnuts and fold them into egg white mixture. Drop from a teaspoon onto ungreased, white paper placed on a baking sheet. Garnish with the reserved walnut halves. Bake at 350 degrees until firm and very lightly browned. Makes 30 small macaroons.

** ** ** ** **

Richard Stockton (1730-81) was born at Morven, the family estate in Princeton, New Jersey. He was yet another heroic signer of the *Declaration of Independence* as well as a member of the Continental Congress. This son of a wealthy land owner was captured in November of 1776 and imprisoned under brutal conditions at Perth Amboy, New Jersey, and then later in New York. The vengeful British beat, tortured and starved him in a futile attempt to force him to betray his country. Stockton was finally released in a prisoner exchange sometime in 1777. As a direct result of terrible British savagery, he was by then an invalid and died at the early age of 50. Stockton was a true American patriot who believed in the cause of freedom so fervently that he willingly sacrificed everything in order to see it come to pass. Regarding his faith, Stockton declared: " ... *I think it proper here, not only to subscribe to the entire belief ... of the Christian religion ... remember, that the fear of the Lord is the beginning of wisdom!"*

Sour Cream Cookies –
A Christmas Favorite of Jefferson Davis

2/3 cup brown sugar	¼ tsp salt
1 egg, well beaten	¼ tsp cinnamon
1 cup heavy sour cream	¼ tsp nutmeg
2-1/4 cups flour	½ cup butter
½ tsp baking soda	½ cup pecans, chopped
1-1/2 tsp baking powder	½ cup raisins, chopped

Blend in a large wooden mixing bowl the brown sugar, beaten egg and sour cream. In a separate mixing bowl sit together the flour, baking soda, baking powder, salt, cinnamon and nutmeg. Cut in butter with a fork. Now combine the mixtures and thoroughly blend. Add chopped nuts and raisins. Grease some baking sheets. Drop batter from a teaspoon onto baking sheets. Bake at 350 degrees until cookies are a delicate brown. Makes about 6 dozen 2-1/2 inch cookies.

** ** ** ** **

Jefferson Davis (1808-1889), President of the Confederacy and former West Point graduate, was a hero in the South during and after the Civil War. After his capture near Irwinville, Georgia, by a Federal cavalry detachment on May 9, 1865, the editors of *Harper's Weekly* were thirsting for blood: *"Jefferson Davis must be tried for treason. If convicted he must be sentenced. If sentenced he must be hanged."* They as well as numerous others in the North were full of hatred for a truly great and Godly Southern gentleman. Yes, Jefferson Davis was a man never to be forgotten in American history. He was an individualist, a moral man, a man of strong character and conviction, and a Christian. While in prison, his reading matter was limited only to his *Bible* and his *Episcopal Prayer Book*.

Soft Ginger Cookies –
Nathan Hale Ate These as a Boy

6 to 8 cups flour	1 cup sugar
1 tsp salt	1 egg
1-1/2 tsp cinnamon	2 cups molasses
2 tbls ginger	2 tbls vinegar
¼ tsp nutmeg	4 tbls baking soda
1 cup butter	1 cup water, boiling

Sift together in a wooden mixing bowl 6 cups of flour, salt, cinnamon, ginger and nutmeg. In a separate mixing bowl, using a fork, cream the butter and sugar. Add egg and beat until light. Stir in molasses and vinegar. When well blended, work in flour mixture from first bowl. Now dissolve baking soda in cup of boiling water. Add this to mixture. If necessary, work in enough additional flour to make a soft, pliable dough. Grease baking sheets. Drop dough from a teaspoon onto baking sheets. Sprinkle with sugar. Bake at 350 degrees for 8 to 10 minutes. Makes about 100 plump, spongy 2-1/2 inch cookies.

** ** ** ** **

Nathan Hale (1755-76), a young Christian patriot, was a true American hero during the Revolutionary War. He was just 21 when the British executed him as a spy on September 22, 1776. Hale had bravely volunteered for a dangerous mission behind enemy lines. Fully aware of the consequences were he to be captured, the youthful and idealistic young army captain went ahead anyway out of love for his country. Nathan Hale bravely went to his death by hanging in an apple orchard. One of the last things he requested was a *Bible*. Incredibly as this may seem, his request was denied by the British. His last words were: *"I regret that I have but one life to give for my country."* In a journal written by British Lieutenant Mackenzie it was reported that Hale *"behaved with great composure ... saying he thought it the duty of every good officer to obey any order given him by his Commander-in Chief ... "*

Maple Nut Christmas Cookies –
As Mrs. Hopkinson's Made for Francis

½ cup butter	3-1/8 cups flour
1 cup maple syrup	2 tsp baking powder
1 egg, well beaten	1 tsp salt

1 cup walnuts, chopped fine

Cream the butter in a wooden mixing bowl. Add maple syrup and beaten egg. Stir together. Sift the flour, baking powder and salt in a separate mixing bowl. Add these ingredients to those in first bowl and blend everything thoroughly. Lastly work in the chopped walnuts. Chill dough for 1 hour. Then roll out on lightly floured board to about ¼ inch thick sheet. Cut into cookie shapes with floured cookie cutter or upside down drinking glass. Lay on greased baking sheet. Bake at 400 degrees until a delicate brown. Makes 8 dozen 2-inch cookies.

** ** ** ** **

Francis Hopkinson (1737-91) was another brave signer of the *Declaration of Independence* from New Jersey. This great Christian patriot was also a poet and a talented song writer as well as an inventor in his day. He and Benjamin Franklin were close friends for many years. Hopkinson is credited with designing the Stars and Stripes in 1777. John Adams' cold blue eyes took the measure of every man in attendance at the signing of the *Declaration*. Not always one to be flattering, he characterized Hopkinson as having a head *"not bigger than a large apple."*

Christmas Nuggets –

A Holiday Favorite of Aaron Burr

2-1/2 cups flour	¾ cup butter
½ tsp baking powder	¾ cup sugar
¼ tsp salt	2 eggs, well beaten
½ tsp cinnamon	½ pound raisins

½ pound walnuts, chopped

Sift together in a wooden mixing bowl the flour, baking powder, salt and cinnamon. Using a fork, work the butter into these ingredients. Then add sugar, beaten eggs, raisins and chopped walnuts. Blend everything thoroughly. Grease some baking sheets. Drop dough by teaspoonfuls onto baking sheets. Bake at 350 degrees for 10 to 15 minutes. Makes about 4 dozen 2-inch cookies.

** ** ** ** **

Aaron Burr (1756-1836) served with distinction in the Continental Army during the Revolutionary War. He was later to become Vice-President of the United States under President Thomas Jefferson from 1801 to 1805. A professed Christian, Burr gained lasting fame and a bit of historical notoriety when he mortally wounded Alexander Hamilton in a duel. He was later charged with treason, but was formally cleared of the charge. Nevertheless, Burr fled the United States and lived in Europe for a number of years.

Sugar Cookies –
James Andrews Favorites at Christmas

1 cup butter	4 cups flour
2 cups sugar	4 tsp baking powder
1 tsp vanilla	¼ tsp salt
	1 cup milk

Cream butter and sugar in a wooden mixing bowl. Blend in the vanilla. In a separate mixing bowl, sift together the flour, baking powder and salt. Add this, alternately, with the milk, to the butter mixture in first bowl. Blend everything well and set aside to chill for 15 minutes. Then roll out on a lightly floured board to a 1/8 inch thick sheet. Cut into cookies with a floured cookie cutter or an upside down drinking glass. Lay cookies on greased baking sheets. Bake at 400 degrees for 10 to 12 minutes. Makes 12 to 13 dozen 2 inch cookies.

** ** ** ** **

James J. Andrews was an Union Army Captain who gained lasting fame during the Civil War when he led a group of his men on a daring excursion against the Confederate military. This young Christian leader and his small detachment of soldiers stole *The General*, a locomotive, on April 1, 1862, in an effort to cut the all-important Confederate rail lines. But these Union soldiers were eventually caught after a long chase by another locomotive, *The Texas*. Nonetheless, the *Andrews Raiders* as they were later called, became famous in Civil War lore for their daring deed on that April day in 1862.

Index

About The Author

Robert W. Pelton has been writing for more than 30 years on a great variety of historical and other subjects. He has traveled extensively throughout the world as a researcher and has published hundreds of feature articles and numerous books. Pelton lectures widely, has appeared on many television shows, been a guest on a large number of radio talk shows, and has at one time even hosted his own radio show.

With the unique biographical sketches found in his historical recipe books, he clearly shows how America was unquestionably begun as a Christian nation. He proves beyond doubt that our Founding Fathers – Jefferson, Franklin, Washington, Hancock and the rest -- left no question as to their personal beliefs in the *Bible*, the Creator, Salvation and the hand of Providence in the development of out great country and the guidance of its leaders from the very beginning.

Pelton has been in demand as a speaker to diverse groups all over the United States. Tom R. Murray of the Council of Conservative Citizens, after hearing him speak a number of times, offers this: *"Mr. Pelton puts together rare combinations of intellectual energies as a writer and speaker that will captivate all levels of an audience."*

He may be contacted for speaking engagements at:

Freedom & Liberty Foundation
P.O. Box 12619
Knoxville, Tn   37912-0619
Fax: 865-633-8398
e-mail: cookery@earthlink.net

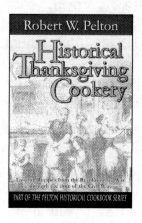

Historical Thanksgiving Cookery contains the recipes for dishes enjoyed by many Christian signers of the *Declaration of Independence* and heroes of the *Revolutionary War*. Also to be found are the favorite dishes of Christian men and women who wore both the Blue and the Gray during the *War Between the States*. Included is a recipe for Benjamin Franklin's **Molasses Pecan Pie;** the tasty **Tomato Relish** so often enjoyed by the great General Robert E. Lee; Thomas Jefferson's marvelous **English Plum Pudding**; and those wonderful **Sweet Tater Flapjacks** eaten by Stonewall Jackson. All of these men were know to be devout Christians. Each historical recipe is followed by an enlightening biographical sketch. Illustrated.

248 pages $15.95 + $4.50 S&H ISBN 0-7414-1141-5

Revolutionary War Period Cookery is a collection of unique recipes enjoyed by many Christian signers of the *Declaration of Independence* and military leaders in the *Revolutionary War*. It contains the favorite dishes of numerous Christian figures from the Colonial period of our glorious history. Included are such recipes as the one for Alexander Hamilton's **Blood Bread** dinner favorite; the **Walnut Bread Pudding** so loved by the great French General Lafayette; the **Ale Fritters** as cooked for George Washington; and the **Chicken and Oysters** dish prepared for John Adams. All of these men were known to be devout Christians. Each recipe is followed by an enlightening biographical sketch. Illustrated.

180 pages $13.95 + $4.50 S&H ISBN 0-7414-1053-4

Five or more copies - 40% Discount
Free Shipping on Orders of 20 or More Copies.

Robert W. Pelton

Civil War Period Cookery

PART OF THE PELTON HISTORICAL COOKBOOK SERIES

Civil War Period Cookery contains recipes favored by people who lived and loved and prayed during the period of the tragic War Between the States. Included are the favorite dishes of many Christian men and women who fought for both the Union and the Confederacy. Here you will find such recipes as **Brown Sugar Cookies** eaten by General Ulysses S. Grant; a **Pork and Parsnip Stew** dish enjoyed by Medal of Honor winner, Mary Edwards Walker; the **Molasses Pie** made by the mother of Nathan Bedford Forrest; and that special pan of **Giblet-Cornmeal Turkey Stuffing** as it was served to the family of Abner Doubleday. All of these individuals were devout Christians. Each unique historical recipe is followed by an enlightening biographical sketch. Illustrated.

168 pages $13.95 + $4.50 S&H ISBN 0-7414-0971-2

Five or more copies - 40% Discount
Free Shipping on Orders of 20 or More Copies.